T0147019

Endorsements

"*Bliss Keys: A Practical Guide to Unlocking Your Purpose* is powerful, practical and guides you on your path to purposeful self-actualization and deliberate co-creation. Readers new to the Law of Attraction will find it easy to understand the concept and those experienced in the principle will find new inspiration and encouragement to use it towards creating their dream."

—Mary Morrissey, Speaker, Best-Selling Author, Empowerment Specialist

"Francisca has compiled and integrated many self-help approaches and methods into a coherent program for people who want to address their life issues in a personalized way. Wandering through the self-help shelves in a library or bookstore with little insight or direction can feel overwhelming. Francisca's books provide clear descriptions of ways we limit ourselves and outline step-by-step how we can take an active role co-creating a more fulfilling life. Her memoir *Breaking Out Gently*, is inspiring. Her guidebook *Bliss Keys: A Practical Guide to Unlocking Your Purpose*, and coaching hub are flexible and adaptable so people can tailor the work to their own specific needs. I highly recommend this program for your personal journey of self-understanding and growth."

—Mary Jo Wevers, Ph.D., Spiritual Health Coach, Karmic Astrologer

"Francisca B. Michel's guidebook—*Bliss Keys: A Practical Guide to Unlocking Your Purpose*—is a must read for anyone interested in finally transforming old and stuck emotional patterns. Francisca is leading the reader masterfully and gently through the *Bliss Keys Process*—combining emotional healing, laser coaching, and mind-over-matter teaching—which will ultimately guide you to find your higher purpose and well-being. Be ready to be amazed as you experience true physical, emotional, intellectual and spiritual break-throughs."

—Simon A. Luthi, VP Global Product Management AMEX, Energy Medicine Practitioner

"This program is the fast-track to finding your path and your purpose in life. It was one of the very best investments of my life. It lead me to where I am, which is the best place I have ever been in my life. I could have given up all the schooling I ever had, all of the academic work I ever did for *this* work. This was far more vital to my happiness and my path than any of that ever was."

—Cinnamon Nuhfer, MLHR, Intuitive Healer

"Over my nearly thirty years as a practicing family medicine physician, I have encountered just a few very rare individuals, professional colleagues whom I consider to be true healers. Francisca B. Michel is one of them. She is exceptionally well-trained, skilled, experienced, gentle, empathetic and patient (but persistent) in guiding us from fear to freedom, from self-reproach to self-love, from darkness into light. I speak not only from my professional perspective but as an immensely grateful client, for whom Francisca provided exactly the kind of ruthless compassion that can make miracles happen. This guide book presents her methods in an approachable, usable and undeniably effective step-by-step program that leads the reader ever closer to and able to hear more clearly the quiet inner voice of one's highest self; beyond ego, beyond circumstances, beyond doubt or preconceived limitations. If you are seeking a path to greater happiness and contentment, and true healing of past or current wounds, Francisca will lovingly lead you there."

—David B. Baron, M.D., FAAFP,
Family Medicine, Founder/Owner Primary Caring of Malibu Medical Group, Inc.

BLISS KEYS

A Practical Guide to Unlocking Your Purpose

FRANCISCA B. MICHEL

BALBOA
PRESS

A DIVISION OF HAY HOUSE

Copyright © 2019 Francisca B. Michel.

All rights reserved. No part of this book may be used or reproduced by any means, graphic, electronic, or mechanical, including photocopying, recording, taping or by any information storage retrieval system without the written permission of the author except in the case of brief quotations embodied in critical articles and reviews.

This book is a work of non-fiction. Unless otherwise noted, the author and the publisher make no explicit guarantees as to the accuracy of the information contained in this book and in some cases, names of people and places have been altered to protect their privacy.

Balboa Press books may be ordered through booksellers or by contacting:

Balboa Press
A Division of Hay House
1663 Liberty Drive
Bloomington, IN 47403
www.balboapress.com
1 (877) 407-4847

Because of the dynamic nature of the Internet, any web addresses or links contained in this book may have changed since publication and may no longer be valid. The views expressed in this work are solely those of the author and do not necessarily reflect the views of the publisher, and the publisher hereby disclaims any responsibility for them.

The author of this book does not dispense medical advice or prescribe the use of any technique as a form of treatment for physical, emotional, or medical problems without the advice of a physician, either directly or indirectly. The intent of the author is only to offer information of a general nature to help you in your quest for emotional and spiritual well-being. In the event you use any of the information in this book for yourself, which is your constitutional right, the author and the publisher assume no responsibility for your actions.

Author Photo by André Schnyder and
Cover Photo by Linus Nylund from unsplash

Print information available on the last page.

ISBN: 978-1-9822-1620-7 (sc)
ISBN: 978-1-9822-1621-4 (e)

Balboa Press rev. date: 07/09/2019

CONTENTS

ACKNOWLEDGMENTS

I wish to thank my daughters, Sarah and Abra, and my ex-husband, Sion, for their unconditional love, patience and support throughout the process of writing this guidebook and its companion coaching memoir. I am deeply grateful to my clients for their courage in doing the inner work, their thirst for living their purpose, and for allowing me to be their guide. Special thanks to Shai Magdish for his coaching and cutting edge teaching. I am grateful to Jaclyn Gelb for her Feminine Energy Circle and for providing the space for healing the "feminine wound." Thanks to Matthew Stainner for marketing-directed guidance and for telling me to write this book the moment I completed my memoir. I am grateful to Christian André Schnyder and Jane Moro for helping create the logo. I wish to thank my teachers at The Journey™, Brandon Bays, Kevin Billett and Skip Lackey, as well Mary Morrissey from LifeSoulutions. I am deeply grateful to my father for everything he taught me about psychology and group analysis. Special thanks to Mary Jo Wevers for facilitating many of my processes over the years, and for editing the manuscript. Additionally, to Paige Parsons-Roache for proofreading the book.

For my clients and members of the Bliss Keys Coaching Program.

INTRODUCTION

Bliss Keys: A Practical Guide To Unlocking your Purpose is for you if you are tired of feeling stuck, frustrated, or powerless in any area of your life. It's for you if a higher, wiser, more peaceful part of you is urging you to go to the next level, make your dream a reality, and live up to your potential. It's for you if a sense of urgency is here, and you're ready to do whatever it takes— including "going within."

Going within in coaching/healing lingo means breathing deeply, becoming still enough to identify how you are feeling, and welcoming that feeling—not to dwell on it but to "burn through" it—thus clearing your inner slate. *Going within* includes self-inquiry, being quiet enough to hear your thoughts, and keen enough to listen to the messages that pulsate up like bubbles of awareness from the deep pond of self-reflection. It means getting to know yourself.

Know Thyself, a motto inscribed on the frontispiece of the Temple of Delphi, imperative in form, indicates that *you must look at yourself.* This maxim was later expounded upon by the philosopher Socrates who taught that the unexamined life is not worth living. There is another reason to examine yourself— unless you know yourself, you can not create deliberate change in your life. The famous quote by 13th-century Persian poet and scholar Rumi, "Yesterday I was clever, so I wanted to change the world. Today I am wise, so I am changing myself," speaks to this axiom. From a metaphysical, as well as a mind-body-healing perspective, we know this to be true. Alternative medicine advocate Deepak Chopra, said to discover the cure for cancer one would have to look *within*. Whether you are seeking to cure an illnesses or you are keen on healing your relationships, or improve your financial wellbeing, whether you want to feel more alive, want to save the planet, or wish to bring your dream into reality, you will first need to look inside yourself and learn how to make changes there.

As you get to know your self, you will find that the "Self" has two parts: the lower self and the higher self. The lower self is the self that is run by the ego, which can be needy, insecure, and manipulative. The self that is run by fear, needs to defend itself and doesn't trust that it is connected to something larger than itself. Your higher self is the self that is one with All That Is, and knows its own connectedness with Divinity. Its guidance is calm and collected, never frantic, but wise—that's how you can tell them apart.

The Bliss Keys Program outlined in this book will help you consciously evolve your lower self and resolve unhealthy ego traits—the masks and patterns that limit you. As you practice the exercises in this guidebook and walk the path of sincere self-inquiry you will strengthen your connection to your higher self who will guide you in making wiser choices in life.

Crisis As Opportunity

The inner work in this guide has the potential to transform any crisis or challenge into an opportunity to make your life better than it was before. If your relationship with someone else or with yourself is not working, rather than getting mad, or shutting down, why not open yourself up to finding out why? Rather than blaming yourself or someone else, how about looking at how you are making your life what it is, and investing your energy into changing it—from within? This mindset doesn't leave much room for blaming anymore, but what it gives you in return is real empowerment. The paradox is that when you take responsibility for your life—for your emotions, your physical wellbeing, the quality of your relationships, your finances, in short, for all of it—this attitude sets you free. It might not feel like that at first. It's not easy to stop pointing at others and to start honestly looking at yourself. But I guarantee you when you make this switch and accept that you are the creator of your own reality, and you come out of the habitual negative thinking—the poor me, the gossip, the victim attitude, the drama—and finally start to use your mind and your heart to create what you would love to experience, life becomes magical. All you need is the willingness to apply your thinking in a new way and to open your heart.

It is profound to see people go on this inner path, to see them connect deeply with who they really are. Yesterday, one of my high-achieving clients who has been struggling with anxiety and a fear of being unlovable went through a two-hour mind-body healing process and arrived in the core of his being—in Source. It showed up as forgiveness, determination, freedom, and authenticity. His voice dropped deeply into his stomach when he spoke from this newfound authenticity—the man he really is under the "good guy" mask emerged. These are the highlights of my work, to see my clients resonate in their essence, their strength, their compassion, their personal power.

Go on this inner path for the reason that is bigger than yourself—out of love for your dream, to live your purpose, out of love for life, for your children, or to save what is good. Release what is not working anymore. Grow and become a better person than you would have been without the challenge. Fulfill your purpose. The *decision* to go this route is the most critical part of all of it. Once you decide, you're committing to becoming the best version of you. Use this guidebook to come back into your true self, to grow, to heal—for the highest and best for all involved.

MODULE 0

OPTIONAL PREPARATION

Chaos Into Clarity

Are you clear where you are? Or unclear? If you're unclear or unsure of whether this guidebook can help you, then use this questionnaire to turn confusion or chaos into enough clarity to get started. Answer these questions without overthinking them. Trust your first answer.

Starting now in this module, you will benefit from writing your answers down. From a neuroscience perspective, it has been said that handwriting your goals helps you achieve them. I am providing space for you to write directly into this guidebook. If you need additional space, use a notebook dedicated to this program.

Where are you in your life? In the area of life that is most important to you? Example: *My work environment feels toxic, and I'm undecided about staying or leaving; I have a big goal and am ready to make it happen; My marriage needs help; I'm facing the dark night of the soul and don't know what to do with my life.*

_____

_____

_____

Where would you love to be in your life? What are you yearning for? What are you envisioning? Example: *I'd love to live my purpose and thrive; I'd love to revive my marriage, or end it amicably, and be free to have the relationship I yearn for; I'd love to manifest my big goal.*

_____

_____

_____

Why do you want that? Example: *Because I'd be able to be authentic; Because relationship and family is what matters most to me; Because I want to make the most of my life.*

_____

_____

_____

What is stopping you from getting it? Example: *I'm so busy I don't know how to change the pace; The communication with my partner is not great; I'm always helping others and don't have energy left for my own things. I stand in my own way.*

_____

_____

_____

If you knew that you could make the changes you need to make, and that you had the guidance to help you with that, would you agree that you could change? Example: *Yes, if I knew that I could release all my resistance and fears, I agree I would be able to make the changes I'd love to make.*

_____

_____

_____

If yes, then make a commitment now to use this guidebook, and for more hands-on guidance, the corresponding Bliss Keys coaching hub at BlissKeys.com. Example: *I commit to making the changes that I need to make in my life.*

_____

_____

_____

Congratulate yourself! Acknowledging that a situation or dynamic needs to be shifted is the first step.

Journeywork

Do you have the clarity to choose what goal or dream you want to focus on? If you lack clarity, you may benefit from *Journeywork* before starting the program. Journeywork or *mind-body healing work* can assist you in overcoming the root cause of your indecision and help you to gain clarity. One of my clients who ended up working with me for a little over a year told me that until she healed emotionally through journeywork, no coaching in the world would have helped her. While she was still feeling lost, and in grief about her recent divorce, her slate wasn't clear enough to successfully apply the coaching program to her life and focus on a new dream. She first had to get good with her emotions. Once she did, she went from having no clue about what to do with her life, to finding her life purpose and becoming a sought-after energy medicine practitioner in Santa Monica.

> Until I healed specific emotional and psychological wounds from my childhood, which were buried deep inside of me, and which I didn't even know were holding me back, I couldn't show up for life at my full potential.
> —Francisca B. Michel, *Breaking Out Gently*

Journeywork is a mind-body healing method, pioneered by Brandon Bays—author of *The Journey*. The technique is a combination of other methods including NLP (Neuro Linguistic Programming), emotional release and memory work, soul retrieval, and integration. The key to Journeywork is to welcome the emotion that is here right now, to feel your emotions fully, and to get out of your head—if your head was able to solve your problem you probably would have already been successful at doing so. A Journey process is like a guided visualization, in which you have your eyes closed and are guided by a Journey practitioner to go deeper and deeper into your emotional self. It gives access to your own body wisdom, your body's own healing power. The technique has proven to be successful in healing issues such as procrastination, depression, performance issues, physical issues, even terminal illness. It is being used globally and has been endorsed by authors Deepak Chopra, Anthony Robbins, and the late neuroscientist and pharmacologist Candice Pert, to name a few. For more information about the inner emotional work in this guidebook, go to Module 5.

The Journey technique can also give you access to your own infinite intelligence, your Source. Once you have access to your Source, you can use this state of being to practice *Top-Down-Living*. Coined by author Tania Kotsos, Top-Down-Living is the practice of first feeling how you wish to feel, and then doing all of your brainstorming and decision making from that place of already *being there*. This is the most effective way of creating the life you desire.

Would you like help with this process? Connect with us at BlissKeys.com and choose your level of desired support.

Module 1

Agreement

Before we begin, let's clarify what will be expected of you for this program to be effective. Once you agree to the points listed below, you can get started. Move through this program at your own pace. You're in control of how deep you go. Enjoy!

1. Practice the Bliss Keys Exercises

This program works because it is practical. If you don't practice the exercises and just intellectually understand the content of the book, you will not reap the benefits. You have to practice.

STEP 1: If you agree with this, write and state out loud: "Because I understand that the accelerated co-creation of my dream can only happen when I practice the Bliss Keys exercises regularly, I agree to do them at least for fifteen minutes every day."

_____

_____

_____

2. Be Present to Joy

Becoming a successful co-creator of your life has to do with cultivating a high vibrational frequency. This has to do with your attitude, your thoughts, and your feelings. Most people live their life just getting by, without a lot of joy. They go through their day automatically, reacting to life, not being fully present. "Okay now I have to cook dinner, then I have to take the dog for a walk, then I have to do another chore and another chore, and, oh, finally I can relax." This attitude towards life robs you of your joy and leaves you feeling down. Therefore part of your daily practice includes you breaking out of the monotonous rut.

Get into the habit of becoming fully present in the mundane and noticing that joy is always accessible to you regardless of what you are doing. My friend Jaclyn—host of the feminine energy circles which have been instrumental in my development—told me that she was watering her lawn yesterday and caught herself going over her considerable to-do list. It was causing her to feel stressed, and for her heart to beat faster. She told me that she "stopped and became totally present to the task of watering the lawn. In the color of the grass, Joy. In the smell of the water and damp soil, Joy. In the feeling of the sun on my neck, Joy." The more you choose to do what you do with care, the more these acts of the heart will accumulate, and your life purpose will reveal itself.

STEP 2: If you agree with this, write down and state out loud: "Because I understand that the co-creation of my dream can only happen when I feel my excitement and joy, I agree, every day, to find joy in the mundane by becoming fully present to whatever I am doing."

_____

_____

_____

3. Go Cold Turkey On The Fixing Addiction

As a society, we are hooked on finding problems so we can fix them—in ourselves, in others, and in our life. We have been trained that we need to focus on what is wrong. It is considered a virtue. Unfortunately, this attitude puts you into a never-ending loop of finding more and more problems. When the mind goes looking for issues on a daily basis, it continually focuses on that which it considers not being good enough. And the more your mind focuses on *not good enough*, the more of *not good enough* it tends to find.

To get out of this negative loop, you can either do years of meditation or, a quicker way is to do the peripheral vision exercise, Hakalau. Five minutes a day is enough at first. In Hawaiian shamanic tradition, Hakalau is considered the process of entering an expanded field of consciousness, or meditative trance. It elevates your awareness. What you labeled a problem moves into the background. It reveals that most of your fears are merely illusions of the mind. Try it out now:

1. Think of a problem you have.
2. Lift your gaze to twenty degrees above eye level—the level of your third eye. Look straight ahead. Find a spot on the horizon.
3. While looking at the point on the horizon, expand your vision. Focus on the farthest periphery on the right and left side of you. You should have a 180-degree field of vision.

4.   Try thinking of your problem.

A new client I recently showed this exercise to burst out laughing when I asked him to think of his problem while he was in Hakalau. Realizing that it is impossible to think of the negative while in the expansiveness of Hakalau, he cracked up. The problem and the expansiveness are on two different wavelengths, like on two different radio signals. You can only be tuned to one of them at a time.

Beware. To the mind that is accustomed to looking for problems so it can analyze and fix them, it can feel quite counterintuitive to enter into a state of being where there is no room for the negative. By exercising Hakalau regularly, you train your mind to experience the world in a new way. To *be* in the world in a new way. It may bring up resistance. All your beliefs about the importance of being watch-guard of your life, of protecting you from danger by being on the look-out for possible issues, are being put out of their job.

The myth that "it's worth more when it's difficult," can also make this exercise challenging. I learned the Hakalau exercise from my own life coach, and he confessed to me that when he was first introduced to it, it was difficult for him to accept how simple this technique was. His ego wanted it to be more difficult. It can feel insulting that all your effort to do right by identifying issues in your life so that you can find solutions for them and please others by doing so should be replaced by a simple open-eyed meditation. It feels disempowering. We're so trained to *do* something, now we're being told all we should do is *be*. It can bring up fear, anger, outrage. This can lead to avoidance.

Let's address the outrage that can come up in the form of inner chatter, flared up emotions, or resistance. You may hear your inner critic saying "I won't stop trying to fix the problem, that's irresponsible, selfish, ignorant. I can't do that!" Most of society has been conditioned to believe that the only way to eliminate a problem is to focus all of your attention on it. To fight it, argue with it, analyze it. The idea of just turning your focus away from it is simply outrageous. It feels passive. But it is the hardest thing to do. I am not suggesting to avoid an issue altogether. I am suggesting, instead of turning your attention to the problem, first to change your state of mind. By doing Hakalau, you open into a state of being in which you are not triggered by the problem anymore but instead feel neutral about it, because you are no longer fixated on it. From this neutral place you can then deal with the issue if it's indeed still an issue.

Through exercising Hakalau daily, you make a significant shift in your energetic vibration. We live in a universe that is governed by specific spiritual laws, including the law of vibration (everything is energy) and the law of attraction (like attracts like). It is essential that you elevate your frequency to become a match with the energy of the life you prefer.

STEP 3: If you agree with this, write down and state out loud: "Because I understand that the co-creation of my dream can only happen when I elevate my frequency to match the frequency of my preferred life, I agree to engage in five minutes of Hakalau every day."

_____

_____

_____

4. Be A Vessel For Change

To facilitate accelerated change within yourself, choose to create a vessel where growth is natural. Breathing deeply and slowly, and drinking plenty of water assists this process. These are two requirements for this program to work. You are improving your relationship to change.

Many of you will have had the experience that when you breathe deeply, you are more relaxed, more present, more focused, also more centered, and more connected to your personal power. Later on, in the program, we will be talking about your "True You," the version of yourself who is empowered, being her/his true self. Not limited by conditioning. When you breathe deeply and slowly and continue to practice being joyful by doing what you do with love, you come into alignment with your True You. It is like an actor coming into the state of being so that the role fits. Do not underestimate the power of these simple things. You might think: "How can this be effective? I want to change my entire life! This is too easy to be consequential." No. Not so. By breathing deeply and drinking plenty of water you provide the optimal conditions for accelerated self-change.

STEP 4: If you agree with this, write down and state out loud: "Because I understand that the co-creation of my dream can only happen when I provide an environment for accelerated change, I agree, every day, to breathe deeply and to drink at least eight eight-ounce glasses of water, but no more than one liter per hour."

_____

_____

_____

5. Have One Corner Of Your Mind Open To The Possibility

Is at least one corner of your mind open to the possibility of you changing your life around from within, no matter what your circumstances? One corner of your brain is all you need.

My teacher of the Dream Builder Coaching Program, Mary Morrissey, told me her story. When she was seventeen in the 1960s, she went from being a picture-perfect high school student with excellent grades, and homecoming queen, to an outcast, more or less overnight. Her boyfriend had come home from college over Spring-break and Mary got pregnant. Once she started showing, the school principal said it would give the wrong impression to have a pregnant girl with all the "normal girls." This was the mindset in the 1960s. Mary was expelled and had to finish her senior year at an evening high-school with other outcasts, such as herself.

Several months after her son was born, Mary, then 17, got very ill. One of her kidneys had to be removed. The second one was declining, too. The doctors gave her six months to live. Mary was terrified. The night before the operation, a minister came to pray with her. She said to Mary that she heard that Mary loves her son and also that she is upset with herself. The minister knew about the power of the mind, and the mind-body connection. She told Mary that it is possible she was poisoning herself with her guilt and shame about her choices. She asked Mary whether she could believe that all of her fear, her anger, and upset could go into the kidney that was going to be removed the next morning? And whether she could believe that the second kidney could heal? In the 1960s, knowledge about the mind-body connection was not yet mainstream, and Mary didn't know what she believed. The minister said that if she could have one corner of her mind open to the possibility of healing, it would be enough. Mary could do that. The next morning the bad kidney was removed, and Mary started getting better. Her second kidney improved and Mary continued to get better. Eventually, she fully recovered. The doctors called it a miracle. Mary has dedicated her life to studying how this miracle was possible and to teach others that they too can create miracles in their life by having at least one corner of their mind open to the possibility.

STEP 5: If you agree with this, write down and state out loud: "Because I understand that the co-creation of my dream can only happen when I have at least one corner of my mind open to the possibility, I agree to keep my mind open."

_____

_____

_____

6. Commit

Are you ready to play the lead in your "movie?" Could you allow yourself to be the hero or heroine of your own life? Are you prepared to make a difference, to have an impact? Will you put your name to your dream? Will you give it your all?

If you don't say yes to this role, no one will fill that spot. It cannot be played by anyone but yourself. There is only one *you*. *You* are needed to make your life all it can be. You have to show up for it as your True You. Don't let your circumstances get in the way. You can't allow them to stop you. They are just facts. They are not the Truth of who you are. Circumstances are merely facts that can be changed. That you are a child of this universe, with the capacity to co-create your life deliberately, is a Truth.

STEP 6: If you agree to create your preferred reality, read the statement below. Sign and date.

I commit to doing the Bliss Keys exercises regularly, and to use my thinking capacity in a new way, so that I may co-create, from the inside out, the highest version of life that I am here to live.

Sign: _____ Date: _____

And so it is. Congratulations!

Integrated Online Coaching Program

To support you on your inner journey, I have created an online coaching hub at BlissKeys. com. It is provided to guide you, and to help you to stay focused. The online program includes the teachings and practical exercises found in this book and provides the space for you to share your experiences, to ask questions and get answers.

It is a place where you can interact with me, my team of practitioners, and fellow members in an emotionally safe environment. Inner work requires dealing with your emotions, and it felt essential to provide a space where all emotions are welcome. Here you are guided to meet your feelings and issues in a proactive, healthy way.

We are also offering you access to a network of other practitioners: emotional healing practitioners, body workers, massage therapists, and energy medicine practitioners. These are people I have personally worked with and recommend so you have the support you need to transform your life.

Send us your questions and comments. Connect with us at BlissKeys.com.

MODULE 2

DEFINE YOUR HEART'S DESIRE

To get the most out of the Bliss Keys Program, if you haven't already, get a notebook to write in. In each module, I will ask you questions. Some can be answered on the page on the provided lines, and some you will want more space for—hence the notebook. I suggest you get a pencil to write with, so you can erase and refine your answers as you evolve. Also, I recommend you start journaling. Writing longhand is a useful practice of contemplation and a way of finding clarity. Every time you sit down and let your thoughts onto the page—uncensored—in a stream of consciousness, you purify yourself from the inside out.

What Is Your Dream? ("Your dream" in this context means "Preferred Reality")

Have you allowed yourself to give your dream/preferred reality a full shot, or are you too busy helping others? Do you still know what your dream is? If not, what are you yearning for? If you didn't believe it was impossible, what would you love?

Your soul speaks to you through your longings and your discontents. If you are not happy, and you're yearning for more connection, more fulfillment, more purpose, more abundance, more _____ (fill in the blanks. Example: *Intimacy; Confidence; Independence; Professional satisfaction; Creative freedom*), then the first step is to take that longing seriously. Listen to your yearnings. By looking to how you feel about your life, and to what is missing, you gain insight into your dream and into what is most important to you.

Here is a trick to find out what it is you want: What, when you see someone else doing it, makes you feel jealous? What makes you feel like *you* should be doing that when you look at someone else doing it? This little stab of jealousy is often a clear sign that you are meant to explore an area of interest.

Also, when does time stop for you because you are so thoroughly enjoying yourself? Or when *has* time stopped for you in the past? What are your talents, your gifts?

STEP 1. List your yearnings. What is missing in your life? What do you need to be happy? Example: *I need to assert myself and to have self-respect and take my calling seriously enough to devote time to it; I need to slow down.*

_____

_____

_____

STEP 2. List your discontents. What do you need *less* of to make room for your real interests, your passion? Example: *I need to stop pleasing everybody.*

_____

_____

_____

STEP 3. Open your mind to boundless, expansive thoughts: If age, resources, education, health and background had nothing to do with it, what would you love to do with your life? Example: *I would love to be my own boss and make my own schedule. I'd love to be a public speaker.*

_____

_____

_____

Distinct Tangible Goal or Feeling State?

No wind is favorable to the sailor who has no destination in mind.

Are you clear about what you wish to create? Some of you will already have a distinct, tangible goal or dream, and some of you won't. Both are fine. If you don't know yet exactly what your vision looks like, then start with *how you want to feel* once your dream has manifested. Become crystal clear on this. The exact details of your vision may not be apparent to you yet—or if they are, they may change—but how you wish to *feel* is something that usually stays the same. It is a good anchor, a "True North" that you can set your creating sail to. No wind is favorable to the sailor who has no destination in mind—so it is essential that you have a destination. Let your goal, for now, be the feeling state that you are yearning for.

STEP 4. How do you want to feel once your dream has manifested? What is your "True North" feeling state? Example: *My True North feeling state is gratitude for the love in my heart; It's a feeling of seizing the day—carpe diem; It's excitement and joy about living my dream.*

_____

_____

_____

STEP 5. Describe why you want to feel like that. Example: *I want to feel like this because when I do I am not afraid. When I am in my True North feeling state I am filled with love and possibility thinking.*

_____

_____

_____

STEP 6. Describe what your life will be like when this feeling state has become your new normal. Make this paragraph juicy, let your mouth water when you read it. Example: *I will get up in the morning with a smile, eager to start that day; I will have the confidence to dress, walk and talk like my "Highest Self," the inner freedom to speak my truth, and the means to turn my vision into reality.*

_____

_____

_____

STEP 7. Imagine yourself three years from now, from a perspective of your dream life already having manifested. See yourself describing to a friend what your life is like now. Feel your excitement. Really believe right now that you're living a life you love. Start your sentence with: "You won't believe what has happened in the last three years..." Now vividly describe your dream life. You can jot down the keywords of your dream life, and then write it into a paragraph.

_____

_____

_____

_____

_____

_____

_____

_____

_____

"Generic Dream" Vs. Heart's Desire

Feel what it is that your soul needs, and what you would love—not from a place of fear, but from love.

Beware, because some of your longings are not your true longings, not your soul's longings. They are ideas of what you *think* will make you happy that are coming from your mind that fears that you won't have, or be, enough.

This happened to one of my clients, who found out that the "dream" she had been living, wasn't coming from love, but from fear. When she got married twenty years ago, her decision to tie the knot came from a place of needing a sense of identity. Being married to someone "important" filled her with purpose. Besides, it took the pressure off of her to make something extraordinary of *her own life*. She married a remarkable man instead and made it her mission to make him happy. These are not bad things. A marriage like that could work perfectly, as long as it's in alignment with your soul's purpose. For my client, it wasn't. Her fear-based reasons for getting married eventually caught up with her. She did a lot of inner work to release the grief that had accumulated over the years—the pain of not living authentically. She came to realize who she really is beneath the fear, and what she needs to be in integrity and at peace.

When you feel anxious and thus needy of: 1.) safety and security, so you never have to worry again, 2.) power, so you never have to feel insignificant again, or 3.) adoration, so you never have to feel unloved again, these desires are not coming from your soul, but from your fearful mind, and your wounded self.

The perceived need for safety, power or adoration can be so strong that it can trap you for years—your whole life even. It can be the reason for staying focused on goals that are not in harmony with your purpose. It can cause you to remain stuck in toxic work environments, in dysfunctional or unfulfilling relationships, or drive you to accumulate excessive wealth, while potentially ignoring the needs of your own soul, and others. When you are operating from within a trap that is held in place by your own fear, this path will keep you wanting more and more. You will never feel satisfied.

STEP 8. Check if your dream is coming from a place of love or from a position of needing to "be someone" so you feel legitimate. Write about it.

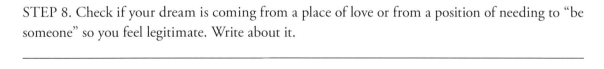

I experienced this in my own life. Although my authentic dream entails scriptwriting and filmmaking, at the time my mother was diagnosed, my script writing wasn't coming from a self-empowered, authentic place yet. I was still trying to prove something, to "be someone," to be worthy. Basically striving to justify my existence. Then, when my mother found out she was sick, it woke me up to come back to a more honest part of myself: where I already felt whole, where I had something to share. This part of me was the one who knows that you can heal yourself from within. This wake up call initiated my decision to becoming a healing practitioner and life coach, and lead me to facilitating mind-body healing with hundreds of people from all walks of life over a course of eleven years, instead of trying to justify my existence by writing the perfect script—when I really didn't have much to say yet. Ironically, following the path of living my purpose, lead me to write two books, one of which may be the source for a screenplay.

To test your dream and see if it's coming from your soul so that you can be sure that it will give you the satisfaction that you desire, ask yourself why you want it. If the primary reason is that you feel insignificant without it, you are probably dealing with a fear-based desire that is motivated by lack. If your dream, however, is coming from an inner call of giving your gift, you are most likely driven by your love, and in harmony with your purpose.

STEP 9. Self-inquire about why you want your dream. Is your yearning coming from a fear of lack, or is it coming from love and the desire to exercise your passion?

_____

_____

_____

It used to feel scary to me to surrender to my soul's purpose. When I investigated that fear, I realized that I lacked trust that the universe had my best interests in mind. Can you trust that life, your Higher Self, "the universe," or whomever you feel has ultimate power, will have your back? Can you believe that you will be safe once you follow your heart and decide to live your purpose?

STEP 10. Contemplate, and then answer these questions: If you already had all the security, admiration and power that you could ever want, who would you love to be, and what would you love to do in your life? What would you do, not because you have to, but just because you would love to do it?

_____

_____

_____

STEP 11. Have you had a wake-up call of any kind? Has something thrown you off balance? Has an accident, or health situation, or any other change in any area of your life jolted you out of your normal rhythm and could be considered a wake-up call? Have you received wake-up calls and did not heed them? And then they became louder? If so, what does it want you to wake up to?

Listen to your gut feelings in answer to these questions: Are you on your right path? Do you need to slow down? Speed up? Change direction? Where do you feel you need to go? What do you need to pay attention to?

_____

_____

_____

STEP 12. Choose a goal or a dream. Regardless of whether you are clear yet on what your ultimate dream, and purpose is, choose now the area of life to focus on until your vision or mission reveals itself. It can be a goal such as "more confidence," or "my marriage," or "career."

Complete this sentence: I choose to make _____ the focus of this program.

Core Values

To test if your chosen goal, or dream—if you already have one—is right for you, check if it's in harmony with your *core values*. Your dream has to be in harmony with your core values so that you can be in harmony with your dream.

If this brings up any resistance, welcome it. (In general, always embrace resistance or any other emotion, when it comes up. As soon as you appreciate the emotion and allow yourself to feel it, or observe it, it usually dissipates.)

What are your core values? What is driving you? What is most important to you in your daily life? What do you value most highly? What do you still need to do in your life? What will please you—one day looking back on it? When people come to the end of their life and look back, it's usually not about the material possessions, but about whom they loved.

When you examine your core values, also explore which of your core values you feel you *should have*, and which ones are authentically yours. What do you live for? Did you grow up believing being a nice girl or a nice boy was most important? Has that value changed over time? Is it more important to be true to yourself, and approve of yourself, than being liked and approved of? Or are you finding yourself in between? Are some of your authentic values still in the closet because you feel there is no safety or support if you unleash them? How would it feel to follow your soul's call? To be that authentic? What would it feel like to be playful, lighthearted, filled with the warmth that comes from having found your purpose and delighting yourself and those you care for with the beauty and power of who you indeed are?

Core Values Exercise

STEP 13.

1. Make a list of all the things that are most important to you now in your life. For example, for your business your list of core values may look like this: *Purpose; Integrity; Success; Inspiring Change; Helping others; Creativity; Passion; Focus; Efficiency; Clarity; Truthfulness; Cooperation. Dependability; Reliability; Loyalty; Commitment; Open-mindedness; Consistency; Honesty.* If you're working on your relationship, your list of core values may be: *Self-Love (in order to have a healthy, loving relationship with another human being, you must first learn to love yourself); Trust; Honesty; Communication; Connection. Happiness.*

2. Prioritize the five most important values and write them down here or onto a fresh piece of paper.

3. Prioritize their importance, placing the most important one at #1. (You will notice that as you move through this program, your core values will move their position of importance according on what you are currently focusing on.) Copy this list onto a fresh piece of paper and keep it visible as a reminder of what you are currently focused on.

Core values #1-5:

1_____
2_____
3_____
4_____
5_____

4. Next, circle one or two core values that stand out as the most important ones to focus on right now, so you know what you're working on. If you're unsure, close your eyes and breathe deeply into your lower stomach. Ask yourself "What core value do I focus on?" Let the answer come to you from your gut—not from your thinking mind. Check if your answer coincides with your common sense and that you prioritize taking care of your basic needs. For example: *Purpose and Success.*

5. Examine, how satisfied you currently are in that area of life. On a scale of 1 to 10, with 10 being deeply satisfied.

Satisfaction Level
(from 1-10, with 10 being completely satisfied, and 1 not being satisfied at all)

Today _____

1 month _____

2 months _____

3 months _____

4 months _____

5 months _____

6 months _____

6. Come back to this question of how satisfied you are once a month and see how you are progressing.

7. Imagine what it will feel like when you are fully satisfied in the area of your life you've chosen to improve!

My mother used to say, "It's not as much about *what* you do it's *how* you do it." She meant that if you do what you are doing with love, with care—when you do your best as opposed to dragging your feet—you find satisfaction, even fulfillment in it. Richard Rudd, the author of the self-help tool *The Gene Keys*, writes that when you do what you do with love, all those acts of the heart build up and begin to pave the way for your life purpose to reveal itself.

Assess Your Dream

For your dream to be the right one for you, it must harmonize with your highest purpose in life.

STEP 14. Assess if your dream is in alignment with your purpose. Ask yourself:

1. Is my dream coming from my heart, is it driven by love as opposed to fear?
2. Does it cause me to evolve and grow?
3. Do I need help from a Higher Power?
4. Does my dream genuinely benefit others?
5. Does it align with my core values?

You want a *yes* to all of these questions. If you answered *no* to any of these questions your dream is not worthy of you. If you have answered *no* to question 5, your idea is not worth pursuing. The inner conflict of it not matching your core values would not be overcome and would either cause you to sabotage your efforts, or would get you what you want—only to find out it's not what you really wanted. For example, if you're a new parent, and your core values include *being present to raise your child*, then taking on a job opportunity abroad that separates you from your infant for several months at a time will probably not be a good fit.

If your purpose, your dream is still clarifying itself in your mind, use these mind-joggers to help you:

STEP 15. When, in the past, have you had the experience of being a vessel, a conduit for something beautiful—larger than you—to come through you? _____

_____

_____

_____

When have you been driven, on-purpose, directed by a connectedness to something, an idea, a knowing?

_____

_____

_____

If you need or want to get in touch with your creative self, I recommend doing the 12-week course *The Artists Way* by Julia Cameron. She too speaks about the benefit of doing "Morning Pages"—three pages of journaling longhand in a stream of consciousness every morning. This will get your creative self to pop back into your life if you have been missing your "inner artist."

How can we help you? Connect with us at BlissKeys.com. Send us your questions and comments.

Module 3

Identify Your Own Truth and Who You Really Are

You are what you believe you are.

Your attitude determines your frequency, which determines your quality of life.

Your Identity

Who are you? What is your identity?

Who you are, and how you think of yourself plays a huge role in what you attract into your life. To illustrate this, here's a teaching story from one of my clients, Emma, who recently changed careers. She used to be a successful production designer, but after some significant life changes, she created a clothing line. Emma has been having difficulties getting production in the factories flowing smoothly. The process feels inefficient, so much so that she is questioning whether she is on the right path.

In her coaching session, I ask her to remember a time when she felt utterly passionate and clear about her identity, professionally. When Emma was a production designer, she tells me, she was in her element. She felt important and influential. Time would stop for her. She didn't need to sleep, it didn't matter whether she was single or in a relationship, she was just happy.

In contrast, now, doing the clothing line feels *weak*. Emma reveals that she has no clear identity right now. She often doubts herself and feels a lack of self-esteem. It's the complete opposite of how she used to be as a production designer. I ask her to imagine taking *the energy* from the time when she was a production designer and *transferring it* to the clothing line. It's time to clarify her own identity and to make sure that the key ingredients that are important to her—feeling powerful and in her element—are included in the new identity that she is creating. Until her character is clear to her, the universe is going to have a hard time giving her what she is asking for. This makes total sense to her, and her energy lifts.

Emma reveals that going through life as production designer felt very masculine to her. Her new career feels feminine. She is not accustomed to doing business from that angle. I suggest that she let the two parts of her, the masculine production designer and the feminine clothing line creator, have a conversation with each other—and together find a new identity that is truthful, that feels effortless, grounded, and real. In this exercise of both parts talking to each other, Emma discovers that the masculine part of her and the feminine part of her can easily support, even compliment each other. She is relieved. Already in her next coaching session one week later, she reports that a new order has come in, and the communication with the factories has become much more comfortable, confirming that she is on the right path.

STEP 1: Let yourself feel who you currently are and who you would love to be. You can draw from other versions of yourself, from different times in your life. You can pull from those experiences any positive aspects that used to work great for you.

Make a list of all the things that used to make you feel that you are in your element. Include in the list the key aspects that need to be a part of your identity for you to be content. What makes you? Who are you? What is key to you? Write about it.

_____

_____

_____

Now, as an exercise, articulate what you are *not*. Not to dwell on it, or hush up the negative, but to find your essence by eliminating all that it is not. Complete these sentences:

I don't like _____

I don't want to _____

What I would never want is _____

I couldn't _____

I wouldn't be fulfilled if I _____

Now, use these mind joggers to *remind yourself of your true identity.* Complete these sentences:

I am in my element when I _____

Time stops for me when I _____

I love _____

I live to _____

It's easy for me to _____

It doesn't feel like work when I _____

When I _____, I feel whole.

If I didn't believe it was impossible I would love to _____

Self-Image: You Can Not Outperform Your Self-Concept

Self-image is defined as the idea you have of your abilities, appearance, and personality. Wikipedia says "Self-image is the mental picture, generally of a kind that is quite resistant to change, that depicts not only details that are potentially available to objective investigation by others (height, weight, hair color, etc.), but also items that have been learned by that person about them self, either from personal experiences or by internalizing the judgments of others."

You can not outperform your self-concept means you can not exceed who you think you are. Simply put, it says that you can not do better than what you think you can. It's all about what you believe. If you think you can, you can. If you think you can't, you can't. So the place to put your attention and to make changes or improvements is on the *thinking level*, the level of your beliefs and definitions.

You can not succeed at creating the life you want if you feel less than the person who you will be in that envisioned life. This means that you have to create the image of yourself, and the belief in yourself, that matches the person you would most love to be.

STEP 2: Instead of allowing your mind to chatter with negative self-talk, stop. Tell yourself you can panic later, and shift your focus onto one thing you love about yourself. Complete this sentence: *What I love about myself is...*

_____

_____

_____

Who does your heart and your Higher Self want you to be? (For example, *My Higher Self wants me to be kind, strong, open, determined, transparent, and to lead by serving.*) Start the sentence with: *My Higher Self wants me to...*

_____

_____

_____

_____

_____

How do you feel about the possibility of creating the life your heart desires? Write your answer down. Start the sentence with: *The possibility of creating my heart's desire feels…*

_____

_____

_____

_____

_____

How do you feel about being the person your heart desires you to be? Start the sentence with: *How I feel about being the person my heart desires me to be is…*

_____

_____

_____

_____

_____

Do you have at least one corner of your mind open to the possibility of becoming the person you dream of being? Because that's enough to start. Are you open to being the person you dream of? Write down your thoughts.

_____

_____

_____

_____

_____

Authenticity

Do you feel you are your authentic self? Do you speak your truth? Do you mean what you say and say what you mean? What about in your environment? With the people you live with, and work with, are you showing up as the Real You with them? Is there anyone you are truly authentic with?

STEP 3: Write down your thoughts. Start the sentence with: *Being authentic…*

_____

_____

_____

_____

_____

If you feel that you can not safely be authentic in an area of your life, but you yearn for that quality, integrity—and relief—that is something to address.

Do you feel that you are not allowed to be your true self? If so, this self-limitation will block you. Do you have a self-image of being shy, of hiding from life, but you want to share yourself with the world? If so, you will have to allow the self-image of you *being visible* to *replace* the self-image of being hidden. To accomplish that, choose to redefine your self-concept so that the beliefs and definitions you have about yourself coincide with who you'd love to be. We will do that in Module 7.

STEP 4: Are you keeping yourself small? Smaller than who you really are? If so, why do you think you're doing that? How is it benefitting you?

It might seem like a contradiction that there should be any benefit in keeping yourself small. Are you afraid of what would happen if you were big? Are you afraid of your passion, your power? Are you afraid of admitting to yourself what you really need, including emotionally?

Write your thoughts down. Start the sentence with: *How I feel about being small or big, weak or powerful, is…*

_____

_____

_____

_____

STEP 5: Birth Order: Do you have a particular position in your family of origin—like first, or second child in line? Has your positioning of first or second born, the middle child, or the youngest child, given you a specific role to fulfill? If so, how do you feel about that? Is that role allowing your true self to shine? Write your thoughts down.

_____

_____

_____

_____

If you would like support with this part of the program, go to the integrated coaching hub and network at BlissKeys.com.

Your Higher Self

Do you believe you have a Higher Self? Wikipedia states that "Higher Self is a term associated with multiple belief systems, but its basic premise describes an eternal, omnipotent, conscious, and intelligent being, who is one's real self." Can you get a sense of *your* eternal, omnipotent, conscious, and intelligent self? Or is that too much to ask?

Wikipedia goes on to say that "each and every individual has a Higher Self. (...) The Higher Self is generally regarded as a form of being only to be recognized in a union with a divine source." The word *divine* may already pose a stretch for you. "In recent years, the New Age faith has encouraged the idea of the Higher Self in contemporary culture, though the notion of the Higher Self has been interpreted throughout numerous historical, spiritual faiths." It goes on to say that the idea of a Higher Self is present in Christianity, Buddhism, and Hinduism.

My perspective aligns with that of most New Age literature, which—Wikipedia continues, "defines the Higher Self as an extension of the self to a godlike state. This Higher Self is essentially an extension of the worldly self. With this perspective, New Age text teaches that in exercising your relationship with the Higher Self, you will gain the ability to manifest your desired future before you. In other words, the self creates its own reality when in union with the Higher Self."

Signs that your Higher Self is in connection with you, or that you are operating from your Higher Self are

- Being in contact with your intuition, receiving hunches.
- Having an "observer perspective," seeing your ego-driven reactions, and gently smiling at them instead of identifying with them.
- The laughter that comes from being able to take yourself and life lightly.
- Considering the long-term effects before reacting from ego, and choosing long-term benefits over instant gratification.
- Having a win-win attitude to life, knowing that there is enough to go around.
- Having healthy boundaries, and being in your integrity, knowing you are your own person and not needy of co-dependency patterns.
- Taking emotional responsibility for your life and choosing to be grateful for everything that has brought you here.
- Choosing compassion for another over fighting and the need to be right.

If you find it hard to relate to this part of yourself that is connected to Infinite Intelligence, to the Divine, it might have to do with beliefs you have about this part of life, or even to the word *divine* itself. What is your relationship with the Divine? You might choose to call it a different name. What about Life Force, or the Infinite Intelligence that created this planet, this universe? What would you call it? You can choose any name for it that you feel comfortable with. I would just like for you to acknowledge that this higher power exists.

Angels can fly because they can take themselves lightly.

—G.K. Chesterton

The Divine

When I was first introduced to the Journey method, the mind-body healing technique that thrusts you into the arms of your own Source, I had to confront my, up until then unresolved, skepticism about anything that was related to the Divine. My main reason for my suspicion was my knowledge of the Middle Ages, and what happened to women who had knowledge, and therefore power during that time, who were burnt at the stake as witches. My antagonism was related to the role the Church has played in the Inquisition. In my unexamined mind, words like *divinity* and the violent acts in the name of God by the Church were associated with each other, and my own pure connection with divine consciousness was tainted.

I surely didn't believe in angles back then because that seemed childish and dumb. There was a link between divinity and angels, so I felt that believing in divinity meant that I was naive and blind. I lived in Berlin, Germany for four years after I graduated from high school, wore mostly black, and worked for an art photographer assisting during his art-photo shoots. I believed in making perfect black and white prints as efficiently as possible, which was my job, and being paid 750 Marks a month, being invited to a nice Italian restaurant, and ordering pasta and a glass of wine at the end of the hard work days. I had no need for words like *divinity*, not to mention *God* at the time. I made pieces of art—passionate sculptures out of clay—when the impulse came through me like a wave that couldn't be stopped. Art was always a part of my life. I saw divinity in art, in life, and would let it take hold of me and flow through me. But I wasn't conscious of it and didn't give it a name.

STEP 6: What is your relationship with the connection to All That Is with Life Force, with Infinite Intelligence, with the Divine? If you are unclear, go on an internal exploration and write down all that you associate with it. Start your sentence with: *What I associate with the words Divine, or Infinite Intelligence is…*

_____

_____

_____

What religion or faith were you raised in? What relationship did your parents have with religion and what beliefs did you take on from them? Was God a man with a beard in the sky? Was he a punishing God? Would you surely "go to hell" if you believed in him? Did it make more sense to you at the time to create distance from all that "nonsense" and avoid the subject altogether?

Here's a personal anecdote. My parents didn't baptize me. They wanted me to be free to make my own decision as far as my faith was concerned. My father completed a Ph.D. in Theology to become a minister. He then completed another Ph.D. in Sociology and subsequently became a university professor of Social Psychology and Sociology. My mother had been a devoted Christian growing up, traveling the world as part of the Australian Student Christian Movement. She developed to become more spiritual than religious. Both my parents were raised Protestant. As I said, they did not baptize me—I made that choice myself later at the Presbyterian Church of Hollywood. On some level, I had always believed in a higher power. When I was about nine years old, I would pray to God every night to keep my parents together—offering up my happiness and everything else I could think of in return as a bargain—with my little hands pressed together. I would pray myself to sleep during those early years.

Being baptized and becoming a member of the Presbyterian Church of Hollywood at age thirty-five had the secondary benefit of getting a discount on their pre-school program my daughter attended at the time. When I grew up, saving money was the highest priority at home. I was raised by my mother to consider the cost of things and to save, to think laterally and be ingenious conserving and saving even more. The belief behind it was that this behavior was necessary to survive. That perspective was more prominent than any other. It had taken over. It had claimed virtue. Could I go as far as saying that *saving* had become my mother's god? Hand in hand with that was a "needing little" thinking. Less is more. Think small, and you'll be better, loved more. Save. Save. Save. I'd stand in front of the bakery window contemplating whether or not to indulge in a seventy-five Pfennig (cent) pretzel. The usual answer was: *No, I don't really need it.* Abstinence from pleasure was ranked highly too. A joke one of my Presbyterian mother's friends told us all one dinner was "Why don't Presbyterians make love standing up? Because it could lead to dancing." My mother laughed so hard, tears came. But she mostly remained loyal to that mindset.

STEP 7: Contemplate. What ranked highest in your life growing up? And what ranks highest now? Depending on the culture you've been raised in, either education or material success—or conversely, modesty—might be the top priority for you.

Is your connection to your Source part of that equation? If your connection to your Source is not ranking highly in your awareness, do some self-inquiry about that. Your connection to your own Infinite Intelligence is going to be of help to you on your path to creating your desired life experience. The more you can come to accept that you are not doing life on your own—but that you are being breathed right now by an Intelligence that has your best interest in mind—the easier the co-creating of the life you desire will be. Journal about it: Start your sentence with: *What ranked highest in my life growing up was...*

_____

_____

_____

Continue with: *What ranks highest now is…*

_____

_____

_____

Contemplate on: *What ranks highest—when I am completely in my element—living my purpose is…*

_____

_____

_____

The definition of "the divine" is *providence or God*. The meaning of the noun *providence* is: 1.) the protective care of God or of nature as a spiritual power, 2.) God or nature as providing protective or spiritual care, and 3.) timely preparation for future eventualities. I would like you to start thinking about *providence*. The use of the word *providence* peaked two hundred years ago, hit a low point in the year 2000 and is slowly increasing again. Can you entertain the thought that you are spiritually cared for by a spiritual power?

I don't know if I can believe that I am being protected by a spiritual power. However, I know for sure that I have been protected, numerous times, by my Higher Self, or something non-physical, energetic, omnipotent. I have had several situations in my life where I was saved by an inner voice that came out of nowhere. Once it happened when I was twenty-two years old and had fallen into the waves on the coast of Bari, South Italy. I was there with my German boyfriend and a theatre youth group from Berlin on an exchange with an Italian theater group. Standing at the edge of a shallow cliff, I saw my boyfriend standing across from me where the cliff was higher—getting ready to jump in. It would have been foolish of him, possibly fatal. There was no way of knowing what kind of rocks were hidden beneath the waves. I could see in his body language the need to prove something. I am not sure if I wanted to distract him from jumping in—I can only remember thinking *how hard life is when you still have so much to prove*—but I stared into the ocean in a trance and let myself fall down the shallow cliff into the water.

I was swirled around by the waves. The bubbles in the clear saltwater were beautifully lit up with rays of the sun. As I was twirled around by another wave, a voice told me, *hold on to the rocks the next time you're pushed against them if you want to live*. I did. The sharp rocks cut the skin on my torso, but I held on. My boyfriend was stunned and couldn't move. He had seen the whole thing. A young Italian man who had also seen me fall, came running, offered his hand and pulled me out. He asked if I was okay. I nodded, shrugging it off, uncomfortable about drawing attention to myself or having anyone fuss over me.

I had at least two other instances where I escaped car accidents, and one incident in which I stayed utterly unharmed in the only, but very dangerous, accident I've ever been in. There have been moments that should have gone wrong, where I felt a non-physical presence watching over me, telling me to look up just at the right time, guarding me, keeping me safe.

Instances such as these are remarkable. They confirm to me that there is another power at play in life. Whether this protection is coming from my own Higher Self or is a sign that there is indeed a benevolent spiritual power looking over me, is unclear to me and that is okay. I don't have to know how electricity works to use it. It is the same with this higher power. I don't have to understand how the non-physical Higher Part of me, my Higher Self works, but I can include her in my life. Letting her in, I stop being on my solo-trip.

STEP 8: If you were protected by a spiritual power, what would that mean for you? First of all, can you believe this? If yes, why? What are some experiences you have had with Infinite Intelligence and with being protected by a higher power? Start the sentence with: *Some experiences I've had when I felt protected by a higher power, were...*

_____

_____

_____

_____

_____

If you can not believe in a higher power, do you know why? List your skeptical or oppositional thoughts.

_____

_____

_____

_____

_____

What do you believe? How do you think your beliefs make you operate in the world?

_____

_____

_____

_____

_____

My question to myself is, *what will happen if I tap into this connection again now, deliberately, and go into dialogue with it and ask for what I truly desire?* Up until recently the old god of smallness and needing little dominated my thinking. But now, I can pick and choose how much smallness I want, and where I allow grandness to come in. Requiring little is perfect in some areas of life when it comes to being happy without grandiose riches, therefore finding it easy to share future riches with those in need. But grandness or at least boundlessness is necessary to be able to allow your vision for your highest destiny to be remembered.

STEP 9: What would a healthy relationship between you and the Divine, or whatever you choose to call it, look like? How would you define it so that it feels right to you?

Write your thoughts down. Start your sentence with: *A healthy relationship between myself and the Divine would feel like...*

_____

_____

_____

_____

_____

The Real You

In her book, *The Adventure of I,* Tania Kotsos talks about Top-Down-Living, "which is living life from the vantage point of the Real You while using the power of your will and intuition to direct your mind and attain your desires." Kotsos brings meticulous research to her book. *The Adventure of I* is an excellent resource for anyone who likes an in-depth explanation of how the co-creative process that I talk about in this coaching program works. The Real You, Kotsos describes, "is the You that is identical with, or at least connected to your Higher Self."

STEP 10: Give this *You* a name now. Do you want to call it your Highest Self, your Higher Self, or your Real You? Give it any name you choose. Complete the sentence: I call the ultimate version of my self my _____

As you continue with this work, you will come to see that this "Highest You" is more in charge of your life than you may think. She is an extension of the infinite intelligence that is making your heart beat, pumping blood through your veins, and making your hair grow. If you can free yourself from all the reasons that resist your Highest Self running your show, in other words—if you can quit standing in your own way—then you can fully embody your Highest Self, and create your dream from that mindset.

STEP 11: Can you get a sense of this Highest You now? Notice if your posture changes. Your breathing. Is it slowing down? Are you breathing more deeply? Are your shoulders relaxing, because

Francisca B. Michel

your Highest You doesn't have reason to be tense and anxious? What does your Highest You know that you don't? Write down your thoughts.

_____
_____
_____
_____
_____

If you feel that there is a big discrepancy between you and your Highest Self, or if you can not get a sense of your Highest You at all, then it just means that you still have limiting beliefs about yourself that are keeping you smaller than what you have the potential to be. Write about it. Start your sentence with: *Where I feel I am not my Highest Self is…*

_____
_____
_____
_____
_____

Can you allow yourself to be your True Self? Are you stopping yourself from moving forward out of fear of what might happen if you did? Is there still something that you are avoiding doing, or that you are avoiding giving yourself permission to feel or think about? What would be the consequences of this radical self-acceptance in your life? Write about it. Start your sentence with: *To fully allow myself to be my True Self would mean…*

_____
_____
_____
_____
_____

Because, as mentioned previously, you can only be what you *believe* you can be, it is important to release your limiting beliefs and replace them with ideas that harmonize with your Ultimate, True Self. (Go to Module 7 for guidance.)

Would you like guidance on how to change your beliefs? Connect with us at BlissKeys.com and choose your level of desired support.

30

MODULE 4

FRAME YOUR OUTCOME

What does your True You need from you?

Begin With The End In Mind

When you write a film script or a book, you soon find out that it is essential, to begin with the end in mind. You must have an understanding of what the ending will look and feel like, or else it'll be impossible to know what you need to include in the story, and what to leave out. If you write with no idea of what the end will be, the writing process will be inefficient.

It's the same when it comes to co-creating your life. Knowing what is most essential for you, knowing your intention, will enable you also to see what you must include now as you are seeding and creating it. What to add in your thinking, in your planning, and especially what to leave out. If you want to harvest apples, you need to plant an apple tree and nurture it until it bears fruit. A lemon tree or an orange tree will not do. If you want to shine in your own right, you need to be authentic, speak your truth and dare to be noticed, not hide in someone's shadow.

Framing your outcome, starting with the end in mind aligns your intentions, thoughts, and actions with your desired end result. If you want to have a peaceful relationship with someone, then fighting over menial things will not be part of your practice. The same goes for your relationship with yourself. If you want to have a peaceful relationship with yourself so all parts of you can be in unison and co-create your dream together, then needing to hold on to grudges or insisting on having to be right won't serve you.

Here is a personal anecdote as a case study: I knew that I needed to change the dynamic in my marriage and most likely get a divorce. I also knew that I could only be happy if my husband and I stayed friends while moving through the process. This was not so much out of a need to keep the peace—which could easily have been a trap that someone with my personality type, "the

Peacemaker," could have fallen into—but from a decision to preserve that which is good for the highest and best for the entire family.

When we first separated, my husband and I were a long way away from a friendship. To begin with the end in mind, I thought of what it might look and feel like to have that desired friendship with my future ex-husband. To get a sense of that, I first needed to become crystal clear about the *outcome* that I wanted. I anchored the feeling of what it would feel like to be separated, divorced even, and remain friends. It felt like a near-impossibility at the time, but I knew that if this is what my heart told me I needed to do, then it would have to be done, and *could* be done.

I didn't know *how*, and I didn't need to know. You don't need to know *how* you will make something happen. In fact, it is not up to you to *make anything happen*. It is up to you, though, to know *what* it is that you truly desire, and to understand what that desire, once it has manifested, feels like.

Once I anchored the feeling inside of me, I asked the high-quality question: *What will it take for my husband and me to get an amicable divorce and be friends?* In response to that question, I received information: thoughts, awarenesses, insights, which told me that to achieve my goal I would have to become financially stable enough to pay for my own way.

This information provided revealing, also somewhat shocking insight that the fear I was facing of becoming independent, of going out into the world and making a living, was something that my husband had been facing already for years! I, for the first time in my life, got a real sense of the pressure and the burden of being a breadwinner. This deeper awareness made it possible for me to empathize with my husband's role, and feel the pressure he was under. It brought me closer to him and made it easier to respect his point of view. It also enabled me to feel admiration for him. Having a broader perspective and a deeper insight into where he was at made it possible for me to stop blaming him and start taking responsibility for my own life, my own moods, my personal circumstances. I caught myself feeling more empathetic towards him because of this more profound understanding of his burden. This new perspective made it easier to imagine what a friendship with him would feel like, which in turn helped me to come into the feeling state of my goal of being friends, despite the divorce.

High-Quality Questions

If you feel stuck in your life or in a situation, it means that your *thoughts* are stuck. It is impossible to frame your outcome and start with the end in mind—so you can streamline towards success—if your thinking is stuck in limitation. Through asking the right *high-quality question*, you will access the ideas and hence the solutions you need. The key is to quit letting past experiences limit or thwart your possibility thinking. Instead, find the answers you need by tuning into the infinite intelligence system that you are a part of.

Albert Einstein (1879-1955) said that we can not solve a problem with the same kind of thinking that created the problem. To find a solution, we have to change our thinking. A high-quality question can do this for you. It can open your mind to new thoughts, unthought thoughts, unthought territory. The act of thinking new thoughts is creative. It entails the willingness and the forward motion of hope, or positive expectation. When you ask a high-quality question, you feel and think yourself into a new, preferred reality.

STEP 1: Ask yourself this high-quality-question: *If I didn't believe it was impossible, what would I love?* Write about it.

_____

_____

_____

Do this for yourself right now. Focus on a goal that you have, and let yourself feel how it will feel once your goal or dream has manifested. Let yourself feel that good. Or if you are in conflict, explore how you would love to feel once this conflict is resolved. Then ask yourself a high-quality question that is already tuned to the end-result you wish to attain.

To clarify how to do this, here is another case study from my own life. I don't like it when my kids' dad goes overseas on long movie shoots. It's happened too many times. I much prefer him in town to help with the co-parenting. Whenever he mentions that he is going away again, my body reacts with a feeling of stress, even panic, recalling the burnout, the workload. This happened a couple of years ago, and I successfully used the high-quality questions technique to frame my outcome and become clear on what needed to happen so that I could come out of the situation feeling positive and not like a victim, depleted, or like a doormat. This is how I got out of victim mode through the use of a high-quality question.

I noticed my thoughts. I saw my victim attitude, that "life is happening to me" and remembered that I do not have to be a victim. I know I can not thrive while in victim mode. Would I rather be right stuck in victim mode, or happy and let that old mode go?

I asked the high-quality question: *What would it take for these months without my kids' dad to not just be bearable, but great? What would it feel like for it to be an enriching experience?* (Please notice that inherent in the question already lies a high-quality answer. In other words, the question is phrased in a way that the answer that this question will attract will be a solution to the situation.) And lo and behold, only moments after I posed the question, an idea popped into my head.

Einstein once said that if he had one hour to figure out a life or death question, he would take fifty-five minutes to find the right question, and five minutes to receive the answer because once you have the right question, you can solve the problem in five minutes. The answer to my question that landed in my head was the idea of having someone live with us, who could help me out while my husband was overseas. Once the idea was formed, I let myself feel for a few uninterrupted minutes at a time what it would feel like once it had eventuated. I stayed open to receiving hunches, or signs, and again, almost instantaneously, I had an inkling of some friends to contact. I followed the notion, feeling positively unattached, and carried out what my intuition told me to do at once—which was to reach a specific friend and tell her my intention. Before I knew it, within a couple of days, an introduction was made via Skype, and a plan was in place. We would have a young woman, a friend of a friend, stay with us. It worked out exceptionally well. In fact, it turned out to be the best three months my kids' dad had ever been away!

STEP 2: Try this out for yourself now: Focus on a goal and let yourself feel how it will feel once it has manifested. Let yourself feel that good. Breathe deeply.

STEP 3: Now that you know what your desired end-result is, identify what is standing in your way of achieving it. What is your obstacle? Write it down.

_____

_____

_____

For example, you might be wanting to lose weight. So the desired end result in the above exercise would be you *feeling and looking trim and terrific.* The obstacle might be that you love ice cream and tend to eat it before you go to bed. To phrase a high-quality question that will offer you the solution to your problem, it will have to include your desired end result, such as, *How can I become trim and terrific while still enjoying ice cream?* Then open your mind to receiving answers. An answer that might pop into your head could be, *I can still enjoy ice cream, I'll just eat it earlier instead of late at night, so I have time to digest it.*

STEP 4: Now phrase a high-quality question with your desired end result in mind.

_____

_____

_____

> If I had an hour to solve a problem and my life depended on the solution, I would spend the first fifty-five minutes determining the proper question to ask, for once I know the proper question, I could solve the problem in less than five minutes.
>
> —Albert Einstein

Would you like guidance on how to use high-quality questions to get out of being stuck? Connect with us at BlissKeys.com and choose your level of desired support.

Deliberate Manifestation Is Simple But Not Easy

To frame your outcome, here is an overview of deliberate co-creation and what you have to look out for, to be successful.

> **Creating your heart's desire in life is simple**
> **When you are in harmony with your vision,**
> **You take inspired action,**
> **Consciously and unconsciously open to receiving,**
> **Fully expecting it to happen,**
> **With patience and gratitude for the highest and best for all.**

Let's break this statement down, thought by thought. I will systematically offer perspectives on how to address each aspect. The more you study the elements of this statement and do the inner work so you can master what is asked of you, the more powerful a co-creator you will become.

Creating your heart's desire in life is simple, means that the exercises that put you into the right mindset to create the experience your heart yearns for, are not rocket science. They are do-able. What can make it challenging, is not the doing of the exercises themselves, but the *resistance* that you may have to apply them.

Your heart's desire means your heart is involved. The goal or dream means something to you. It is not a sudden idea. It's something you want to be "married" to. It's something that comes through you when you are your true self, following your bliss.

When you are in harmony with your vision, means the dream you are envisioning harmonizes with your Real You, and with your soul's purpose. Or, at least, it is in alignment with—and a stepping stone to—living your life's purpose. This requires taking into consideration the truth of who you are and of who you are not. Your longings and your discontents, and your core values in life.

You take inspired action means the action you're making towards your dream is in sync with the cyclic energy (passive/receiving, active/giving) that is coming into and out of your experience. It means you engage in brainstorming, and follow your hunches towards your dream. Your action is inspired, not pushed. You're weaving your journey of life, rather than controlling or manipulating it (see Module 10).

Consciously and unconsciously open to receiving, means you are entirely in. All the voices in your head unanimously agree that they want to create the goal or dream. Even your unconscious thoughts are on your side and are not sabotaging you. Limiting beliefs of not being good enough, or not deserving, have been released (see Module 7).

Fully expecting it to happen, means you're not shy, or embarrassed about admitting your dream. You fully believe it's going to happen. It's not some crazy, out-there idea that feels too good to be true. You are comfortable with the dream being your new normal.

Most people have not been raised to expect their dream to happen. Your parents most likely did the best they could with the resources they had, but your parents can not give you what they have not been given or haven't successfully provided for themselves. But just because you weren't trained to believe in your dreams manifesting doesn't mean it can't be done. It just means that you have to let go of the stories that keep you in the past, let go of the blame that defers responsibility, and let go of the fear of change that keeps you in your comfort zone. It just means that you have to be proactive about it.

With patience means that you are whole and complete within yourself even while you are waiting for your dream to fall into place. Also, that you are able to hold your vision in an open hand without clenching, or feeling desperate for it. It means to be committed to it, but not needy of it. You have given up attachment, as in the Buddhist teaching, knowing that attachment to an outcome produces suffering. Attachment actually pushes the dream away. It is as if a higher intelligence is saying, *I will give your dream to you, but only once you have come into your center, and you know that you are already whole and complete just as you are.* You have mastered the art of being focused on your dream, but healthily unattached.

Gratitude, means you approach life with gratitude. You're grateful for all that has brought you here. You have made peace with your past. You have blessed it, along with all the pain, all the lessons that made you who you are today.

For the highest and best for all, means that the achievement of your dream benefits you as well as those you care about.

As you go through the program, you will identify what is required of you to be successful in creating your dream. Lean into the areas that feel difficult.

You have to be determined to make the inner changes you decide to make. You are up against your lifelong habits and perhaps your environment. If your habits are keeping you small, and your environment makes you feel incapable of living your full potential, then you have to become deliberate with yourself and with life. Fearless like a tiger who defends its cubs, you need to protect your destiny from the mediocrity or negativity of your limiting habitual thoughts. Better yet, befriend your fear, since you are not a tiger.

Fear will be present whenever you are at the edge of the life as you've known it, signaling that you are pushing the envelope. Fear is actually an indication that you are pushing the boundaries of your life. Good for you!

Send us your questions and comments. Connect with us at BlissKeys.com.

Module 5

Focus Your Manifesting Mojo or 'Art of Allowing' Skill

Accept yourself unconditionally.

Create a Gap

Most people operate by default, automatically, without conscious awareness. Your phone beeps and you immediately pay attention to it, you get triggered, you react. You get an email and you respond. Somebody says something, and you answer. Someone cuts you off in traffic, and you react—depending on your temper. This is an unconscious way of being alive. It is a reactive way of being alive. There is no personal power in being reactive. To change this, let's create a gap. Unless it's urgent, practice delaying your responses. This will help you become aware of what's going on in you and in your reality. The delay creates a gap. Becoming aware of the gap will become a tool. In the last phase of this program, you will shape your reality by how you perceive it, and how you respond to it.

There might have been an incident where you became conditioned to respond to life in a certain way. An authority figure might have expected you to take a particular path. You might have opted to abide by the expectations, or to rebel against them. In any case, you might have become accustomed to accepting yourself only when you fulfill others' expectations, or go against them. You may not know what it feels like to accept yourself for who you really are. But your soul is not letting up. It is saying, *I yearn to be fulfilled, to make a difference.* To be able to follow your soul's call, your bliss, you must first take back your right to respond to situations from a centered place. Not automatically, not by default like a robot.

To notice what you're noticing is the single most important self-mastery skill.

—Mary Morrissey

37

By becoming aware of when you are on autopilot in your life, and implementing a gap instead of reacting unconsciously to life, you'll be awake and alert enough to notice what is happening in your thoughts at the moment.

STEP 1: To practice this, start catching yourself operating during your day doing something automatically when you're not present. Just notice that you're noticing it. That's the gap. It's the beginning of taking control of your life from the inside out.

What are the times when you are on autopilot in your life? When you do the dishes, brush your teeth? When you automatically react to what is being thrown at you. Write it down.

_____

_____

_____

Your Perception Changes How It Makes You Feel

Becoming aware of your automatic reactions by delaying your response also makes it easier for you to handle your emotions. Let me explain.

Your emotions—how you feel—is determined by how you think about something. If you believe that something is positive, you will feel good. If you believe that something is negative, you will feel bad. This means that when you train yourself to stop reacting to your circumstances—through a delay—it will become possible for you to determine the moment a strong emotion comes up. Once you notice a strong negative feeling arise, you can change your thoughts on the subject from negative to neutral so that instead of feeling bad, you can feel neutral about it.

To reiterate: Your beliefs and definitions about a situation determine how you feel about the situation. This means that you can change your definitions and your opinions about something that you can't control, to improve how it will make you feel. For instance, right now I can't change the famine in Africa, but instead of feeling paralyzed and powerless, I can remind myself that I am doing what I am here to do—helping in my own way, at my personal capacity. Writing is my sward. I can protect my energies from going into drama, and entering fights that are not mine to fight. It means that you can let go of things you can not control and fully engage in the things you can. By fully engaging, I mean you sign your name to the dream. You're all in. By changing your perception, you change your attitude. It's still just as terrible that children are dying of starvation. Yet because of my altered perception it is not ripping me apart every day. Instead, it helps me stay focused on my specific purpose.

Here is another way to illustrate how your perception changes how you feel. Let's say you're in an argument with your teenage child, or anybody else who has the ability to "press your buttons." The tone in their voice has triggered you, making you feel disrespected, or not good enough. You notice your defenses going up. Your heart rate increases. You recall all the other times you two have been in an argument, and judge them for being "so disrespectful." You gasp and can hardly believe you have to deal with this. You notice yourself raising your voice, or shutting down.

Then you stop yourself, and change your perspective. You remember that you can do this. You remember that once this argument turns into a power struggle, nothing can be resolved, and will make you feel off-kilter for the rest of the day. You remember to put yourself in your teenager's shoes. You give them the benefit of the doubt and entertain the possibility that they are not intentionally disrespectful, but that they are coming from an entirely different perspective. You change your attitude from needing to be right to being curious. You drop your defenses and ask them what they meant by saying what they said. You find out that from their perspective they feel x, y and z. You realize that they had no intention of being rude towards you, but that they feel under a ton of pressure and have a lot of stress and want you to acknowledge all that they are doing, and not expect more from them than they can manage. You realize that what you thought was a disrespectful remark is actually a request for help, and that their tone of voice is not personal. You understand them and feel a sudden wave of compassion for them. Suddenly and unexpectedly, you hear yourself asking how you can best support them. You feel your anger melting. You feel warm and full of love and gratitude for this shift. What made this shift possible? The fact that you were open to hearing and feeling where they are coming from—their perspective, and accepting the possibility that they weren't out to intentionally hurt you.

The same dramatic shift in how you feel and think about yourself is possible by changing your thoughts about your life and about yourself. If your current beliefs about yourself are making you feel small, then implement a gap, i.e., stop yourself from reacting automatically. Instead of going down the negative spiral and ending up in self-doubt or self-loathing, change the beliefs you have about yourself. (More on how to change beliefs in Module 7.)

STEP 2: Implement specific changes right now. Self-inquire how your perception of yourself is causing you to think and feel about yourself. Do you have negative thoughts that make you feel a certain way about yourself? Write about it. Start your sentence with: *Negative thoughts that make me feel badly about myself are…*

_____

_____

_____

Think of one thing you love yourself for. Plant that firmly in your mind. What can you say to yourself, from a place of integrity, to help you shift your perception about yourself in your favor? Begin your sentence with: *One thing I love myself for is…*

_____

_____

_____

To be more appreciative of yourself, what is one thing that you will either stop doing to yourself or that you will start doing for yourself? Write about it. Start your sentence with: *One thing I will stop doing to be more self-appreciating is…*

_____

_____

_____

Then: *One thing I will **start** doing to be more self-appreciating is…*

_____

_____

_____

Emotions Transform Mind Into Matter

It was mentioned in Module 3 that your self-image is derived either from personal experiences or by internalizing the judgments of others. To determine where you have internalized judgments from others or where personal experience has left marks that are holding your self-image down, look to how you feel about yourself. Your emotions are a reliable thermometer of whether or not you have unresolved personal experiences or internalized judgments.

Emotions are energy in motion. To focus your manifesting skill, you need to free the power held in your feelings. To do that you need to come into a good relationship with your emotions. Entering into good contact with your feelings is not only important for health reasons—repressed emotions have been said to be the emotional root cause of cancer and heart disease—feeling your emotions is also important because your emotions carry your energy through your body. On a biochemical level, your emotions are the *messengers that communicate with the body-mind*. In her book *Molecules of Emotions - Why you feel the way you feel,* the late neuroscientist and pharmacologist Dr. Candace B. Pert defines emotions as being "cellular signals that are involved in the process of translating information into physical reality, literally transforming mind into matter." What this means is that if you are still weighed down by unresolved emotional issues, you can not help but bring some of that heaviness into your daily creation. If you want to live your destiny, free and clear from past hurts and limitation, you must learn how to deal with your emotions healthily.

Some emotions, as stated above, will change, just because you stop yourself from automatically reacting. By getting more information on a subject, you gain a broader perspective, change your attitude and, as in the example above, your anger can turn into compassion.

Other emotions, however, those that are stuck in your body from the time you experienced childhood trauma, for instance, or those that are flowing through you because of a loss, those emotions need to be fully felt. We all carry pain, not just our own pain, but a collective pain in our bodies. Depending on how sensitive you are, you will feel this pain as a form of underlying anxiety, fear or sadness.

The only way to free yourself from the heavy burden of feeling this pain is by whole-heartedly welcoming it. Yes, that's right, by surrendering to the emotion, you paradoxically transmute it into pure energy. By embracing the negative sentiment, by allowing yourself to be annihilated by it—it really feels like that—you free yourself from it. You must get good with allowing yourself to feel your emotions without judgment, without the need to fix them, and without running from them. Instead, acknowledge them, like wounded children, and welcome them in an unconditionally loving embrace, as best you can.

The wellness industry talks a lot about being positive. There is a stigma on being negative. As a result, many people shut their negative feelings down and put on a happy face. There is a fine line between putting on a smile with the purpose of letting it make you feel better, and putting on a fake smile and being in denial about how you feel. Stay honest with yourself. Make sure you have at least one person, whether it's your life coach, your best friend, or your aesthetician, where you can be entirely truthful about how you feel. Journaling can also help. Vent onto the page.

The rewards of welcoming all of your emotions as they come up, one after the other, is that they lose their power over you. When you feel angry, and you allow yourself to feel that anger down to its very core, the emotion eventually dissipates, and the energy that was wrapped up in it is then available to you. On the other hand, if you manage the anger in any way other than healthily owning and fully feeling it—if you either repress it, put yourself down, or alternatively direct it outward onto others, or onto inanimate objects—you stay stuck with it.

If emotional issues are not resolved at their root cause level—by going to the original pain and coming to an energetic resolve, such as forgiveness, with the person who hurt you—you have to go through the whole drama again, projected onto different people, in different scenarios, but the same emotional patterns. We can stay stuck with the same patterns for years, decades, even an entire lifetime, if we don't resolve them.

If you have been abused psychologically, emotionally, physically or sexually, it is possible that the shame and guilt from the oppressor or perpetrator were transferred to you, the victim. Because re-living the traumatic event within your memory is scary, you may have found ways to avoid feeling deeply. You're not alone with this. As a society, we are experts at numbing our feelings and running from our pain. People resort to a wide variety of methods to distracting themselves from facing anger, fear, and sadness. People narcotize themselves with alcohol, with shopping, and workaholism, so they don't have to feel the void. People stuff their pain down with overeating or by staying busy. Feelings are held at bay with caffeine, nicotine, and other forms of addiction, including drugs, sex, and social media. Gossip, blaming and complaining also keep feelings down, as well as analyzing and staying in your head. When you numb the negative emotions, however, you also numb feelings of joy and excitement. As a result, you start to live in emotional mediocrity. No deep pain, and no ecstatic joy, just predictable, safe old boring numbness. When you are unconsciously avoiding feeling the pain that you've tucked away, you are not genuinely excited about life, you disengage, and your dream can slip away.

To reiterate: There are two completely different ways of dealing with your emotions, both of which we are using in this program: The first way is to identify the underlying belief or definition that is causing you to feel the way you feel, and to change your thoughts so that they evoke better feeling feelings, as described above. The second method is to explore the emotions down to their very core and let them "burn through you" until they dissolve.

I want to emphasize that the method of fully feeling your emotions to release them is not an invitation to dwell on them or to throw a pity party. This is an invitation to *get good* with your emotions by dealing with them consciously. Feelings are like young children, they need to be acknowledged. So, when you feel genuinely into an emotion when it arises, it's the equivalent of giving a young child attention when it really needs it.

It's not always a sign of strength to toughen up, keep a happy face, and get on with life. Sometimes, allowing yourself to let go and break down is wiser and more courageous than staying strong. Find someone who is not afraid of the truth of how *they* feel to hold the space for you to express your true feelings. If you have no such friends or want to have someone neutral to do that with, any of the Journey Practitioners listed on the integrated coaching hub at BlissKeys.com can help you. One Journey process can have a greater healing effect than several years of talk-therapy because you are bypassing the mind and are dealing with the issue at the emotional root cause level. It is well worth the investment for a one-on-one process.

Pass Through Your Own Suffering

This entire coaching program won't work unless you feel your emotions. You can not get the results merely by *figuring it out*, and by staying in your head. The emotional part of your being needs to be involved. You grow into your Highest Self through breathing and living into that version of yourself. If you have emotional wounds, they might make it hard to breathe deeply, out of fear of what might come up. This next exercise guides you how to do it.

When you let yourself feel your negative (and positive) emotions fully, in a focused manner, without getting distracted by the story that comes along with it, but by staying focused entirely on feeling a pure emotion, you purify yourself from the negativity—or attachment to the positivity—that is in the feeling. This is important for your effectiveness as a deliberate co-creator of your life, since, as stated above, your emotions literally transform mind into matter. The goal is to become so fully accepting of everything that you find inside yourself, of all of your feelings, no matter what they are, that you arrive in neutrality, balanced between the extremes. That is where your real power lies, *in neutral*—aware of the extremes on the positive and the negative side, and content to be in the middle. To arrive there, however, you must first learn to get good with your emotions. (More on neutrality, see Module 7.)

> All the coaching in the world wouldn't have moved me forward until I healed emotionally. I had to let go of guilt, blame, shame. Get good at being vulnerable.
>
> —Cinnamon Nuhfer

Emotional Release Exercise

You know how good you feel after a big cry? This exercise (inspired by The Journey™) can give you the same release for all the other emotions you might face. Not just for sadness or grief, but also for the frustration, the confusion, the resistance, the numbness, the anger, the rage, the jealousy, the self-pity, the self-loathing, the judgment, the guilt, the shame, the anxiety, the fear. The fear of being unlovable, of being abandoned—all of it. There is no emotion that you can not resolve by fully feeling it. This exercise works if you stay with it.

STEP 3: Take a private moment. Find a place where you will be undisturbed for about twenty minutes. Have tissues and a glass of water near.

- Sit spine erect. Close your eyes. Become still.
- Let your mind know that you are safe. Thank it for always protecting you. Ask it to take a back seat, to relax. If it interacts, appreciate it for sharing, and give it the job of making sure that you are breathing deeply.
- Let your heart know that all emotions are welcome, even the shy ones that might have been hiding—afraid to show themselves. Remember some feelings are like scared little children needing unconditional acceptance and love.
- Breathe deeply into your lower stomach. Let your stomach know whatever emotion comes up—no matter how raw— is welcome.
- Focus your awareness on the emotion that is the strongest in your body.
- Welcome the emotion, no matter how subtle, powerful, or uneventful it is, such as numbness or nothingness.
- Breathe and relax into the emotion. This might feel counter-intuitive.
- No matter what emotion arises, welcome it. Identify it, and on a piece of paper jot it down, one word. (When you write it down, continue feeling it fully.) Everything you feel is welcome, even frustration about there being no emotion. Even resistance.

- Surrender to the emotion. Feel into the core of it, into the heart of it, where it is the strongest. Let the emotion wash over you and "devour" you until there is nothing left. You may feel a feeling of death or a void. It might feel intense. Breathe into it. You are doing great!
- Feel if there is an emotion rising up from beneath.
- Welcome that new emotion and feel it fully. Give it the same unconditional welcome as with the feeling that came before. Identify it and write it under the first emotion that you experienced.
- Continue this process and go through all the emotional layers that come up. Once you have burned through all of the negative emotions, you will eventually arrive in an inner state of pure being-ness. It might feel like an expansiveness, neutrality, bliss, love, or something similar. This is your Source.
- Rest in your Source for a few minutes. Bask in its boundlessness. Feel all of your cells recognizing yourself arriving home in this consciousness. This is who you really are at your core.
- Welcome this state of being and take an internal snapshot of it so you can practice tuning into it whenever you choose. Your Source is the most powerful, valuable state of being because it is the place from where you can exercise Top Down Living, mentioned in Module 3 and 10.
- Integration: To complete this emotional process tune into your Source, and then glance at your list of emotions that you fully felt and burned through and systematically wash up through each layer of negative emotion. Your list of emotions may be anger, sadness, grief, emptiness, void, Source. So, say to yourself: "Knowing that I am Source, I now let my Source wash through the void that I felt earlier. I let my Source bathe and dissolve the void until all that remains is my True Self." Next, wash through the previous layer of emotion.
- If your Source has any wisdom to communicate with each layer of negative emotions as you wash through them, write this wisdom or guidance down so you can refer back to it in the future.
- Wash through all the layers of negative emotions until you reach the top layer. Feel how good it feels to know that at your core—no matter how strong the negative feelings may be—there is always Source waiting for you.

If this process gets too much at any point, notice that there is an *observer part* of you. From the observer perspective, you can gain an overview of the situation and distance yourself from identifying with the story in the emotion. Remember the meaning you give it is the meaning it will hold for you. When you remove the *negative connotation* that you have associated with the story, it will be much easier to feel neutral about it.

Taking responsibility for your own emotions by burning through them, as outlined above, releases the energy that is held in them—and brings you into *neutral*, the optimal co-creation state.

If you are not familiar with this process from any other work you have done before, and it feels confusing or overwhelming, that is understandable. This is advanced work and needs practice to be able to conduct it on your own.

Would you like help with this process? Connect with us at BlissKeys.com and choose your level of desired support.

Forgiveness

To truly accept yourself—forgive yourself. The emotional work helps you release deep-seated trauma and clear your slate. To make that emotional work complete, you must sooner or later forgive those you've been holding grudges against. Anger can motivate you to step into action, to stand up for yourself, and that can be positive. However continually being defensive or in judgment mode only holds you back. To optimize your manifesting mojo, you can not hold onto grudges or have a chip on your shoulder. You need to forgive everyone and everything, including yourself.

STEP 4:

- To come to forgiveness, go into a quiet place within.
- Who do you need to forgive? Write your answer down. Start your sentence with: I am willing to forgive _____ so that I can move on.
- Imagine stepping into the being, into the consciousness, of the person you need to forgive. If this feels uncomfortable, or unsafe, imagine a surrogate, an "enlightened mentor," and have the mentor step into the person you need to forgive instead.
- Directly, or through your surrogate, feel what the person you need to forgive felt like at the time they hurt you. Where were they at? Find your answers not from your mind, but from your gut. Breathe deeply and relax. Go as deep as you can. Write down: *The person I need to forgive was feeling* _____
- Can you feel compassion for the person you need to forgive? If so, this might make it easier to release them energetically.
- Check in with yourself: Are you ready to forgive the person you have to forgive from the bottom of your heart? This does not mean that you're condoning their behavior—making

it okay what they did to you—and it certainly does not mean welcoming their behavior again. It just means forgiving them so you can be free to move on.

- If you are ready, then imagine the person you are forgiving and say out loud: "I forgive you." Write down: I forgive _____ from the bottom of my heart, so that I can cut the cord, leave the baggage behind me and move on.

- If you are not ready to forgive, see if you can forgive them partially. Perhaps thirty percent, or fifty percent or seventy-five percent.

- Ask yourself what would have to happen so that you could forgive fully. Listen for the answer and follow the guidance. Complete the sentence: *In order to fully forgive* _____, the following needs to be said or done:

_____

_____

_____

What activity or thought process brings you into your center? What is something you will do more of to feel good, in your essence?

_____

_____

_____

What is something you will let go of?

_____

_____

_____

Would you like guidance? Connect with us at BlissKeys.com and choose your level of desired support.

Module 6

Envision Your Success

Choose to be optimistic, it feels better.

—Dalai Lama XIV

Visualize Your Highest Self—Your True You

Imagine that at your core you are a perfect, radiant being with infinite potential. Some of this radiance has already manifested in your life, and you feel there is more. You may have gotten glimpses of how far you could go.

Because what is inside is outside, what you have the potential to be must already exist as a seed within you, as well as a fully manifested possibility in the universe. Just as a seed that is placed in fertile soil, watered and exposed to light, grows into its full potential, it is in your DNA to develop into what you have the potential to be.

STEP 1: Can you conceive of the outcome you desire in your life? Can you imagine being the person who you will be in that envisioned preferred life? Breathe deeply, relax your shoulders and face and contemplate on these questions.

_____

_____

_____

What would help you become comfortable with the thought of that and especially with the feeling of that?

_____

_____

_____

Francisca B. Michel

Who do you choose to be? What do you want to have? What really matters to you, right now?

_____

_____

_____

When it comes to envisioning your success, imagine yourself three years from now. That gives your mind enough space to accept the idea as a viable possibility. It's all about what you believe. So it makes sense to think about the dream that you're weaving in a way that you can accept it. Three years feels so far out, so much could happen and change for the better in three years. Your entire life could change. You want this kind of mental space for your thoughts and for your imagination to have room to play. Be free in your thinking. You get to choose what in your life you want, so it matches who you really are: self-respect, fulfillment, harmony. Let it in. Let yourself feel it.

STEP 2: Imagine yourself three years from now, reminiscing about what has transpired over the past thirty-six months. Envision telling your friend how juicy your life has become! Abundance? Flow? Oh, gosh, so much of it, so much!

Really get in there. Taste that life. What are you wearing? How does the breeze feel on your skin when you're speaking your truth, when you are reaching out, touching many? (If that's your authentic dream.) When you're at peace? When you're a millionaire? (If that's your dream. You can be a millionaire and still choose a simple life—if that's what is right for you.) Imagine the freedom. The places you have been, the people you've met, the positive influence you've become.

Remember, you are imagining it as if you are looking back on your life, from the perspective of it's already happened. Feel what it feels like to have made, and to be making an impact in the lives of others by being you! Your fully expressed you! With all your quirks and idiosyncrasies, you made your dream come true! Congratulate yourself. Imagine lifting that glass. Party, celebrate. In your gut, in your cells, let that happiness bubble over, put on some music, dance like you will when your beliefs have aligned with your purpose!

Endeavor To Live The Life You Are Imagining

> If one advances confidently in the direction of their dream, endeavoring to live the life they are imagining, one passes an invisible boundary and meets with a success unexpected in common hours. All sorts of things begin to occur that never otherwise would have occurred. New, more universal, liberal laws begin to establish themselves around that person. The old laws are rearranged in one's favor. Nevertheless, one begins to live with the license of a higher order of being.
>
> —Henry David Thoreau

48

Henry David Thoreau (1817-1862) is saying the world will open up to you as soon as you advance confidently towards your dream, endeavoring to live the life you are imagining. This is an immense promise: You believe in your envisioned life and move towards it with confidence, and in return, doors will open, and the universe will manage you! So, what are you waiting for? Imagine your dream! It's simple. Most people just make it complicated.

Because you have to know what your goal is so you can move in the direction of it, it's time now to get ready to write it down into a Vision Statement. Things tend to come in focus when we put them to paper. Focusing on your Vision Statement is a beautiful anchoring of all those day-dreams and yearnings. The act of condensing your vision into words, in itself, is a process of sharp focus. It's a decisive step of manifesting it into material reality. When done with an open heart and from a grateful place, and in connection with your driving passion, your Vision Statement becomes a highly potent tool for focusing your mind and—envisioning the life of your dream.

> I dream for a living.
>
> —Steven Spielberg

Vision Statement

STEP 3: Now that you are getting images and feelings of how much you are going to love your life, let yourself feel it in your whole body. Take it even further and ask yourself: *If I didn't believe it was impossible, what life experience would be the highest expression of my True Self? What is my highest purpose? And how does it feel to be living it? To be it?* Then let that feeling land. Write about it. Start your sentence with: *If I didn't believe it was impossible, the highest expression of my True Self would be to…*

_____

_____

_____

It helps to do this exercise in a place where you feel some reverence and where you have peace and quiet for at least five minutes at a time. You can stretch this exercise and have fun for hours, or you can keep it short and sweet.

STEP 4: To prepare to write the vision statement, breathe into your stomach as deeply as feels comfortable. Come from your gut. Notice images, thoughts, and feelings that come up as you imagine already living your vision.

Breathe another deep breath and imagine how you will feel when your vision has become your new normal. Breathe in again and imagine expanding your consciousness and your "vessel" to make room for so much harmony, beauty, resolve, for so much abundance, joy, and aliveness.

There is a resoluteness in your gut and in your groin when you are fully present and fully engaged in being you, open to receiving, and open to giving. Allow yourself to know what is right for you. Allow yourself to remember.

STEP 5: Take a stab at your vision statement. Write longhand. Resist editing while you're writing, just write, edit later. Write the title: *Vision Statement*. Notice how the act of writing the vision statement feels to you. Do you tense up when you write? Do you feel pressured to come up with something good? Allow yourself to write out everything that comes to mind, get it out of your system. Begin with the words: *I feel happy and grateful now that...*

_____

_____

_____

_____

_____

If you don't know what to write yet, write *that*. Write in a stream of consciousness: *I don't know what to write...* Just keep writing without editing, until your vision reveals itself to you. For example, *I don't know what I want yet. I don't want to make a vision, because I am so involved with the now. If there is anything I'd like, it's to be through with the divorce and having done it in a way that is gracious and has even more love flowing.*

See, now, I'm *in*! Now, I'm feeling the vision, but only because I allowed myself at the beginning to express my doubt or resistance. If you need this, like I just did, do it. You can edit the beginning out later. The more comfortable you feel with this vision statement, the easier it will be for you to get inspired by it and use it to remind you of the dream that you are confidently heading towards.

For example, *It's with gratitude that I write this. I'm in utter amazement about the fact that my kids' dad and I have a friendship now. Our daughters are continuing to thrive. We give them space to blossom and shine in their own right. Our dedication for them allows us to show up at our best. I feel that my life has improved 1000% on all fronts.*

STEP 6: When you feel that you are starting to rave or begin to lose touch with reality, stop, and ground yourself. Resist the temptation to take off on a tangent, or into fairyland, making up a princess or hero story with a life description that you have no connection with. Stand not knowing for a moment what you would love. Let yourself become still. Remember your Source. Feel how you would like to feel. Then keep going, write it all out, edit later.

Remember you're still writing with the perspective of three years from now. For example, *The breakthrough did come, my books got written and published. The coaching hub took off like a wildfire. The time that I knew would happen came. I have the red chair. The cast and crew come to my studio. We work, and we film. It is part of the creative process. It's energetic, playful, moving.*

Here's a bit from my old vision statement. When I read it now, I can feel the old ego's need to be recognized. Here it is: *I have made a name for myself of generously serving with humility, grace, and joy, of being optimistic and magical.* It felt good to me when I wrote it a couple of years ago, as if the words *grace, optimistic* and *magical* were bringing in those qualities, strengthening me in accomplishing that. But now it feels somewhat disconnected from who I am because I don't talk like that.

STEP 7: Rewrite and fine-tune your vision statement until it feels right. For example, *I discovered my innate talent to become quiet and still. From this place of inner peace, I wrote two best sellers. My team and I have been honored with the Nobel Peace Prize for my online coaching program BlissKeys. com. My dream of being a conduit for love in the world has become true.*

It's okay to include things in your vision statement that you feel embarrassed about, or that your mind that is used to thinking small thinks is outrageous—such as stating that the books will be bestsellers and mentioning a prestigious award. If you don't start saying it, however, how will you ever accept it as a reality? When will you stop resisting the good that is meant to come through you? When will you trust yourself to live what you're here for? When will you get out of your own way? Express your truth. For example, *My team and I are engaged in pioneering a life system that honors the feminine energy which leads from tenderness. Gratitude is here. Belonging to my family and my tribe is here. Healing, laughing and dancing is here. Abundance is here. My "Sisters" are here. Creative freedom and exploration are here. Love is here. Passion is here. A new and fulfilling relationship is here. This or something better manifests easily and effortlessly in harmonious ways for the highest and best for all.*

Envisioning your success is having the willpower to think more about what you desire to create and less about what has been your reality up until now. In fact, it means that you *starve* the old fear, the early thoughts of limitation. It means that as soon as you recount the limiting past in your story, that you stop yourself and bring your focus back on that which you are deliberately co-creating. Keep refining your vision statement so that it becomes more and more an energetic match to the dream you are feeling in your heart.

Would you like help with writing your vision statement? Connect with us at BlissKeys.com and choose your level of desired support.

MODULE 7

CLEAR YOUR SLATE

Identify Your Blocks

As stated earlier,

> **Creating your heart's desire in life is simple**
> **When you are in harmony with your vision,**
> **Consciously and unconsciously open to receiving,**
> **You take inspired action, fully expecting it to happen,**
> **With patience and gratitude for the highest and best for all.**

If co-creation is as simple as described above, why are you struggling, or at least not yet fully thriving in some areas of your life? It's mainly because of the self-limiting, false beliefs and definitions that you have about yourself and about your experience. Mostly unbeknownst to you, you have taken on these beliefs since childhood—perhaps as far back as in utero. These limiting beliefs obscure your true self. They restrict your outlook and cramp your thinking. They create a veil, a mask, a shield, a wall, and a suit of armor between you and the life you have the potential to live—your preferred life. Because you attract what you unconsciously believe is the most likely thing to happen—which is usually based on past experiences—it is no wonder that you are attracting a life that is not yet a full match to your highest potential.

There are other factors involved in regards to what you can and cannot be in this life, that are out of your control, such as the destiny of your soul and your physical background. What you do have power over, however, or can learn to have control over, is which conscious and unconscious beliefs you let run your life. Are they self-supportive beliefs, or self-sabotaging beliefs? The beliefs you host control what kind of vessel you are. Are you a suitable candidate for your dream to land in, and to be lived through?

In this module, I will show you how to bring your unconscious beliefs into alignment with your conscious goals and dreams, so that you don't have to sabotage your efforts without even being aware of it. Remember in your gut, with every cell of your being, that you are radiant and allow yourself to show up in the world and live your life from that place.

STEP 1: If you are feeling pushed into the corner by life, if pressure is mounting, use this circumstantial urgency to your advantage. Use it to declare to yourself that you are making a change. Plant firmly in your mind that you are going to improve what has, up until now, been impossible to change.

Real You Vs. Conditioned You

STEP 2: To become conscious of where you currently align with your Real You and where you don't, make a list with two columns. At the top of the right column write the header *conditioned you* and at the top of the left column write *Real You*. Notice that I have left *conditioned you* uncapitalized to imply the smallness that we unfortunately often associate with ourselves.

Real You   **conditioned you**

Please note that even if you drive a big car and live in a big house, or know you will one day, you may still feel small inside. You may look successful, but unless you are content from within without the need for greater and greater possessions, power, admiration or security, you have not arrived in your Real You yet. The Real You has no desire to show off how big it is, how important or how influential. It merely is what it is, connected to everything, to *All That Is,* and that is enough. Your Real You is so saturated with life and Life Force, that it is actually more focused on *being* and *giving* than on getting.

STEP 2 continued: Into the left column under *Real You* write the adjectives that describe the Real You.

If you can't get a sense of this version of yourself yet, that is okay, just wait until you begin to connect with her/him and then come back to this exercise. If your soul is hungry for it and you are willing, a Journey process can put you in touch with your Source and your True You usually within one or two sessions.

Would you like one-on-one guidance? Connect with us at BlissKeys.com and choose your level of desired support.

In the right column under *conditioned you*, write all beliefs that come to mind, which are causing you *not* to resonate yet with your Real You, and hence stop you from stepping into the shoes of him/her consistently in your life. For example:

Real You (adjectives)	**conditioned you (beliefs)**
confident	don't be too confident
upright	pride is a mortal sin
beautiful	don't be more attractive than your sister
powerful	got me killed in another life
sensual	that's unsafe
sexual	that's immoral
brilliant	slowly allowing myself
independent	scary
engaged in giving	need to replenish and conserve energy
expressing her passion	need to create safe space for that

STEP 3: The next step is to look at the negative beliefs under the *conditioned you* column and identify where each belief is coming from. Whose voice is it? *Whose* perspective is it? Did your mother think that? Your father? Perhaps you are merely conditioned to talk in lesser terms of yourself because anything else would be considered bragging and was frowned upon.

If you have held yourself back, or you're in a loop of striving to fulfill others' expectations, write about it here or in your notebook. Start your sentence with: *How I feel about my Real Self is...*

_____

_____

_____

Have you ever noticed that those who are stuck in their life tend to put down those who are about to spread their wings and fly? What do you think this has to do with? Write about it.

_____

_____

_____

Did you have anyone in your life growing up who curbed your passion with scary tales of the world? Or conversely, were you expected to perform, to be the best, causing you to believe that you weren't lovable unless you are always at the top—no matter the price, the sacrifice? We're not going to undo those beliefs yet. We're just going to take notice of them, and investigate what the "benefit" is that you are deriving from them. When you have reaped the information from the old beliefs that you need, then you can distinguish which of them you wish to release. Contemplate on the question whether anyone curbed your passion, and write about it.

_____

_____

_____

To give you an example of how negative limiting beliefs can keep you stuck, here's an anecdotal teaching story. Several years ago when I was working with my own life coach, I finally came face to face with the limiting belief that was at the core of my issue with *not enough money*. It had to do with my mother. I uncovered that I had been copying her insecurity about her worth and around finances to feel close to her, to honor her brilliant creative resourcefulness. This belief had been unconscious, up until then, silently controlling the quality, and expansiveness, of my life. I came to realize that I was drawing love from my old belief, limiting as it was. Loyalty and devotion held it in place.

Until you discover what is at the core of the belief that is limiting you—until you find the good in it, the perceived benefit—you can't let it go. How can you let go of something when you don't know what it is? Letting go happens when you level with the issue that held your limiting belief in place. Deal with it respectfully, without judgment, without the need to get rid of it, but rather with the intention of gently sifting through the good and the bad that the old pattern has been giving you.

In the fairytale, Cinderella has to sort the good from the bad lentils. It is a test. In the Brothers Grimm version, the oldest stepsister says: "You belong in the kitchen where there is a bowl full of lentils. When we return, they must be sorted, and take care that we don't find a bad one among them. Otherwise, you'll get nothing good." There is wisdom in the stepsister's words. If there is one lousy belief in you, one lousy lentil—one voice that forbids you to be all you can be, that says you're unworthy—it will spoil everything. Then yes, it's true, you'll get nothing good.

And who came to the rescue in the fairy tale? Cinderella's helpers: the birds and the mice. What if you too had little helpers who would help you sort through the bad and the good seeds of your beliefs, definitions, and thoughts? What if you didn't have to do it alone? Well, you *have* helpers! Your birds and mice are your intuition, your sixth sense. It, together with your emotions, will guide you to the harmful beliefs and will let you know what to keep and what to release.

Detailed instructions on how to change your beliefs follows. For one-on-one support contact us at BlissKeys.com.

There is an element of surrender when you allow yourself to look at your limiting beliefs and dive down into their core, to their origin. When you go deep into self-inquiry about a subject, you are bound to reconnect with the emotions and thoughts of that time.

In the next segment, we are going to become systematic about releasing your limiting beliefs, and I ask you to do it with self-respect. Know, we are not here to fix you, there is nothing to fix. You are already whole and complete in your core. We are only here to shine a light on the old operating system of your beliefs. We will go about dismantling it with as much consideration for all parts of yourself as needed—including any younger yous. It can be your younger self, your consciousness from that time, that can oppose your current plans. If you don't deal with that one lousy lentil, one limiting belief can spoil everything.

Imagine: Let's say the three-year-old self inside of you had the thought that one day she will marry and live happily ever after. It's an honest belief from her early life. This belief feels familiar and stable, it's become part of her identity. How do you think that three-year-old-toddler-consciousness inside of you is going to respond to your decision to change the dynamic in your relationship that could potentially lead to revoking "happily ever after?" With a tantrum, perhaps? With fear? Tears? With retreat? Hiding from life? All these responses confuse the mind, so it doesn't have to face the issue. In any case, it is unlikely that she will respond with: "Oh, that's fine, go find yourself. If need be, separate or get a divorce. Never mind about the fairy tale—that I have believed my entire life!" So, expect some resistance from within.

STEP 4: Meet any internal resistance with allowing it to be there. Welcome it. Say to yourself: *It's okay for resistance to be here.* When you make it feel welcome, it usually doesn't stay very long.

STEP 5: If this feels scary and you don't feel ready, take heart. Gain leverage over your fear with this Worst/Best Case Scenario Elicitation. Answer each question from your gut.

Fear Elicitation: Worst Case Scenario—Best Case Scenario

What is the *worst* that can happen? Complete the sentence: *The worst that could happen is…*

_____

_____

_____

If *that* happened, what would be the *worst* that would come *from that*? Complete the sentence: *The worst that would come from that would be that…*

_____

_____

_____

If *that* happened, what would be the *worst* that would come *from that*? Complete the sentence: *The worst that would come from that would be that...*

_____

_____

_____

If *that* happened, what would be the *worst* that would come *from that*? Complete the sentence: *The worst that would come from that would be that...*

_____

_____

_____

What would be the *ultimate worst* thing that could happen? Complete the sentence: *The ultimate worst that would come from that would be that...*

_____

_____

_____

Best Case Scenario

Flip your perspective to the possible *positive* outcomes. What would be the *best* that could happen? Complete the sentence: *The best that could happen is...*

_____

_____

_____

If *that* happened, what would be the *best* that would come *from that*? Complete the sentence: *The best that would come from that would be that...*

_____

_____

_____

If *that* happened, what would be the *best* that would come *from that*? Complete the sentence: *The best that would come from that would be that...*

_____

_____

_____

If *that* happened, what would be the *best* that would come *from that*? Complete the sentence: *The best that would come from that would be that...*

_____

_____

_____

What would be the *ultimate best* thing that could happen? Complete the sentence: *The ultimate best that would come from that would be that...*

_____

_____

_____

You can use this fear elicitation to reveal and overcome resistance to doing the inner work. Switching to the positive—the best case scenario—allows you to stretch your possibility thinking into the positive realm.

> To live the life at your full potential, you first have to free your consciousness from limitations that you have accepted as normal.
>
> —Francisca B. Michel, *Breaking Out Gently*

Your Unconscious Mind Is Running Your Show

Let's talk about the unconscious mind since it plays such a prominent role in the subject matter of manifesting the life you want. Even though most people are not aware of this, the unconscious mind is the driver of your life experience. It is the silent director, the one at the steering wheel. What can make life so frustrating at times, is that we are not aware of the power of the unconscious mind. We think we know what we want, and especially if we are being positive and doing affirmations, we've been told that by the law of attraction we should manifest it. But it's seldom as easy as that. Why are we getting so much of what we don't want? Your unconscious mind is the reason why.

Sigmund Freud, (1856-1939), founder of psychoanalysis, described the relationship between the conscious and unconscious mind as the top and bottom part of an iceberg that's floating in the ocean. The part of the iceberg above sea-level is equivalent to your conscious mind. It is what is visible and known to you. The ice underwater represents the unconscious mind. You don't see or understand it, but you depend upon it to carry you. The unconscious part of your mind—more specifically, the beliefs and definitions that are harbored in the unconscious mind—determine what you attract or repel. You could say, the beliefs and definitions in your unconscious mind make up the "programs" that is running your system. They are the "software." You are the "computer."

As most of you know, the software that runs a computer determines the machine's capability. If the software is old and not compatible with a newer application, for instance, you will need to upgrade it to run the newer app. And, you also know, that you *can* upload more up-to-date software to replace the old. You don't have to replace the entire computer every time you upgrade the software.

It's not that different in humans. Your "software" is your unconscious mind. Your "programs" are your beliefs and definitions. They too, can be changed. You just have to know how to access the unconscious mind, and you have to know how to "install a new software." Without this capability, it's like having a computer with one software program that was installed in the first six years of your life—and which you are continuing to use. Can you imagine how limiting that would be? But that is how most people walk through life, with the same programs that were installed in early childhood. By the age of nine years old, most of your beliefs and definitions have been formed based on what you saw and experienced in your youth. That is the basis of your programming.

What if you were born into an environment that caused you to believe x, y and z—and they comprise the programs you are running? But now, you're a grown person with your own life experiences and your conscious mind believes a, b and c. If you are stuck with your childhood programs of x, y, and z, good luck! There is no way you are going to be able to operate a, b and c on your "computer" smoothly. It's going to crash at every corner because your new beliefs are incompatible with the old software. But instead of uploading a new software program, we get stressed, we think there is something wrong with us, we bang our head against the wall, or we blame our mother. No one has told you what's going on. You're not even aware that you have an old program running.

I want to change this for you. You should know how to improve your "computer programs" so you can run your life more effectively. Also, you should know that you can *invent* your own computer program, according to what you want it to do for you.

Once you understand how co-creation works, and how you can succeed at this game, you're going to be able to create any "program" that is in harmony with what you deep down believe in your heart, and wish to manifest. It is the most beautiful way to be alive—you remember that you are a creator. You can update your software according to your ever-evolving dream.

Motivation

"You are always motivated to do what you are doing," my life coach told me years ago. "Then why am I struggling?" I asked. "Because for some reason you're motivated to struggle," he said. That sounded ludicrous, but I could see a possible benefit: Struggling, living month to month, was what I knew. Fear of lack was a mindset I was raised with. My mother grew up in the Australian Depression. There was not enough to eat. Her brothers had to shoot rabbits to feed the family.

Lack—and the fear of it—was the reality she knew. I took that on from her. Even though when I was a kid, my dad had a secure job, fear of lack and thus a mindset of struggle was an identity I could be good at, loyal to. I copied my mum. I was motivated to carry the same weight, struggle together—it makes no sense to the logical mind, but on a gut level, it does. I wanted to chip in, worry too. Find life hard, too—not consciously of course.

"How would you say you are operating in life right now?" my coach asked me. "How are you *motivated* to operate in life?" he added. "I'm *tagging along,*" I said. "To keep the waters calm—I'm *motivated* to keep the peace."

It wasn't anything new to me, even back then, that "keeping the peace" was an old pattern—after all, I was "the Peacemaker," according to the Enneagram Personality Type system that I had learned in The Journey Program. However, I could see where my coach was going with this question. "Keeping the waters calm" was not what my True Self needed. What I really needed was to be *bold* and fully show up for life. To believe in my self enough to go after my vision, even if it rocked the waters a little. I expressed frustration that I hadn't been able to do this yet.

"And," my coach continued, "if you could say that to yourself without an attitude, without frustration or judgment—and simply accept it, accept all of you—that will be good."

Let's reiterate, you are always motivated to do what you are doing, just that all too often you are not aware of what is motivating you. Hence you often get results that you don't consciously want, or that are not in alignment with your highest purpose. For example, you might think that you are motivated to have a fulfilling relationship, but deep down, unconsciously, without even being aware of it, you may be more motivated to copy your parents' dysfunctional relationship dynamic. Why would you do such a thing? Because it is familiar and as such, feels safe. And you are not even aware that you are doing it.

You might ask yourself how you can possibly change a motivation that you are not even aware of having. You do this through a *Belief Change Exercise*, in which you are guided to first *identify* the limiting beliefs, such as the fear of lack, and to become aware of the *benefit* that you are deriving from the old pattern. Each belief change that you do is a deliberate act of letting go of the old way, of the limitations, and the conditioning that is keeping you stuck. Kudos to you for making it this far. Keep going. You're doing great!

Changing Negative Beliefs

Negative beliefs that result in negative self-talk and self-sabotage are "toxic." If you want to be in right relationship with yourself and live your full potential—sustainably—you can't live with a stack of negative beliefs about yourself. The guilt, the self-doubt, the limitations you unconsciously entertain are most likely behavior that you have taken on from your parents or caregivers—shaped in your childhood. Regardless of where they come from, you have to learn to *spot it* and *stop it*.

Give back what's not yours. If you took on fears about life, and doubt in yourself—unaware of the limiting consequences—it is time now to hand these ways of being back to their rightful owner. The experiences you made by making life hard for yourself has most likely given you life lessons, and perhaps even compassion for those who share your pain. Be grateful for that.

Belief Change Exercise

Whatever you find out about yourself, refrain from self-judgment as best you possibly can. If you judge yourself for any limiting self-concept you have, this judgment will glue it to you even more. What you resist persists. So, instead, notice the negative belief and breathe in a deep breath of self-acceptance.

Before we go into the exercise, let me introduce *the mirror concept*: To become crystal clear about the beliefs and definitions that are currently limiting you, use your life *as a mirror*. Because we know from psychology that you create your reality with your beliefs and definitions, it stands to reason that you can look at your reality closely and find out what your beliefs and definitions are. You can look at your circumstances, your bank account, your relationships, your health—in short, every area of your life—and draw from it the unconscious beliefs and definitions that you have about those areas of life.

For example, let's say you are choosing to make improvements in the field of finances. To apply the mirror concept to that area of life, look at your bank statement. If your income is less than what you need to live comfortably, you can derive from that, that your beliefs around finances are something along the lines of

- *Having enough money is hard.*
- *I'm not worthy of living comfortably.*
- *I can't make a living.*
- *There is never enough.*
- *Money doesn't grow on trees.*
- *I'm not a Rockefeller.*
- *It's not okay to have more than others. The list goes on…*

STEP 6: Belief Change Exercise

1. Choose one area of the main areas of life (general wellbeing, physical health, finances, relationships, career, vocation) that you will focus on and improve first.
2. Describe what that area of life is like now and how you feel about it. For instance: Area of life: *Relationship.* How I feel about it: *Okay on the surface, but I feel lonely.*

3. Then, ask yourself: If that area of my life is a direct mirror of what my beliefs are about that area of life, then what must I be believing? For instance: *To have a relationship in which I feel lonely, I must be believing that relationships make you feel lonely.*

4. Now that you have identified the limiting belief—*relationships make you feel lonely*—ask: What is the benefit of the belief? Ask your gut, not your head. The answer may not be logical to your thinking mind. For instance: *What is the benefit of believing that relationships make you feel lonely?*

5. Answer the question. For example, *The benefit of believing that relationships make you feel lonely is that it's what I saw my mother live out in front of my eyes and I didn't have to question her and her ability to live life.*

6. Then repeat the same question and ask: What is the benefit of that (insert the answer from above question)? Example: *The benefit of not having to question my mothers' ability to live life is that I could instead keep looking up to her as a role model, which gave me a sense of security.*

7. Keep asking the same question: What is the benefit of that? And always insert the last answer. Write down the answers. For example, *The benefit of feeling a sense of security is that I felt safe.* (Continue to ask the same question "What is the benefit of that?") The benefit of *feeling safe* is that I felt like *I could rely on something.* The benefit of *feeling like I could rely on something* was that *I didn't have to consider whether it might be better for my parents to separate.* The benefit of *not having to consider whether it might be better for my parents to separate* was that *I didn't have to face the possibility of my father moving out.* The benefit of *not having to face the possibility of my father moving out* was that that *things stayed the same and that I felt special because I had parents with whom I had a special relationship with since they needed more of me since they weren't intimate with each other.* The benefit of *feeling special* was that *I felt needed, that it gave me a place, a role, a purpose - it made me feel worthy.*

8. Then connect the first perceived benefit you discovered, (*believing that relationships make you feel lonely*) with the last benefit you found (*feeling worthy*), and ask yourself: Does that make sense? *Does believing that relationships make you feel lonely, lead to you feeling worthy?* Ask yourself if this is working for you?

9. Then answer. Example: *No, that is not working for me at all. That is not even logical. It's sad and is keeping me stuck in a belief that is keeping me lonely.*

10. Because the old limiting belief is, most likely, not working for you, see if you are willing to let it go. If yes, decide to let it go now.

11. Tell yourself why you are choosing to let it go. For instance: *I am letting go of believing that relationships make you feel lonely and deriving a sense of worthiness out of that because that is not working in my life at all. That old way of thinking is keeping me stuck in a childlike relationship with my parents and doesn't allow me to grow up into an adult and be free to have an adult relationship. I deserve more.*

It can be dumbfounding what you find when you dig down into your unconscious in this way. Meet it all with gratitude and acceptance. You are freeing yourself from unconscious baggage.

By consciously acknowledging that the old belief is not working for you anymore you are unhooking yourself from the need to keep it in place. By letting go of the need for it, you enable yourself to let go of it. You make space inside. Take a deep breath. Acknowledge yourself for the work you just did!

12. Make sure to fill that new space inside yourself with a deliberate new truth that supports you. For instance: *I am open to having a mature, intimate relationship in which I feel fulfilled, met and connected.*

Important: Do not judge the old belief or try to fix it. There is nothing to fix. You are whole and complete in your core/Source. The negative, limiting beliefs are not the truth, they are just thoughts you have been accustomed to for a long time. You can let them go, at your own pace.

If you are unable to make a full-hearted decision to release the old "program," there is a chance that you are still getting more benefit out of keeping things the way they are. The unhealthy ego likes to stay in control and may resist you letting go of the old way. This is why people will often only change once they're being pushed into a corner by life—sometimes of an existential nature.

STEP 7: How long do you want to remain in your current circumstances? Let yourself be honest about it. Write your truthful answer down. *I want to stay in my current circumstances until…*_____

Whenever you notice your limiting belief pop back up, make a deliberate choice that this belief no longer works for you. Deliberately choose what you prefer to believe now and in the future.

Tip: By having your end goal in mind, and knowing and feeling who you ultimately want to be, any unconscious saboteurs (limiting beliefs) that are contradicting your goal will begin to come into your awareness. So, a quick way to find your blocks is to decide that you are living your dream and to move towards it actively.

Important detail: The shift to a fulfilling relationship in the above case study will come from shifting the focus towards the solution of *enjoying* a fulfilling relationship, and *not by being focused on finding* a fulfilling relationship. More on that in Module 10.

Do you have a lot of emotions coming up? Does the issue feel complicated or overwhelming? Would you like help with this process? Connect with us at BlissKeys.com and choose your level of desired support.

Psychological Projection And Blame Shifting

> I learned that I didn't have to project my blame onto my husband or my parents, or anybody. That just kept me stuck. I learned that to be able to let go of all blame, I would have to take complete responsibility for my life—my choices, my circumstances, my emotional wellbeing. If I could take full responsibility for all of it, this meant that I would not engage in any finger-pointing or victimhood.
>
> —Francisca B. Michel, *Breaking Out Gently*

A significant way people stay stuck is by blame shifting. By making someone else responsible for what you dislike, you feel like you're off the hook. This is called psychological projection. Britannica states "projection is a form of defense in which unwanted feelings are displaced onto another person, where they then appear as a threat from the external world. A common form of projection occurs when an individual, threatened by his own angry feelings, accuses another of harboring hostile thoughts."

The problem is that while you are projecting your own unconscious impulses, or shadow, onto others, you cannot simultaneously be fully empowered. You may look and even feel temporarily enabled, but it is a pseudo power that is riding on denial and is usually driven by fear. It is not the empowerment that comes from being in touch with the innate ability of your True Self, and from serving your True Self's highest purpose. While you're involved with this type of unconscious behavior, you cannot attract your highest version of life into your experience. All that you get while you are blaming and judging others is more of the same.

As a rule of thumb, if you are triggered by something, it is yours to deal with. Here is a teaching story from my own life as a mother: I used to get enormously triggered by my kids' clutter. They used to get so many clothes from my mother-in-law, they would overflow out of the drawers, and pile up on the closet floor. I'd say things like "You have to value what you have. How can you even find what you have when it is all so crowded?" Knowing that when I am triggered, it's my issue, I stopped to think what exactly I was triggered by. If my irritation was towards my kids not honoring something valuable, then I had to ask myself how I am not honoring something of value in my life. What am I not valuing in my own life that I am projecting onto my kids? All of a sudden it hit me. I had been writing in journals every since I was nine years old. I have thousands of written texts in diaries and notebooks, on discs and hard drives, on my computer desktop, and in folders. For years they had been unsorted, unvalued, and unpublished. It didn't even occur to me to do anything with them. I was nudged plenty of times by friends to write articles and publish them, but that idea felt foreign, not for me, as if they were talking about someone else. Why was I able to write and write, but not ever do the one thing that would allow it to come together so it could see the light of day and be shared? Why was I holding myself back from contributing to life with my writing? Once I had the clarity to ask this particular question, the answer came spontaneously: It was lack of self-worth. It was as infuriating as it was devastating.

I had to allow myself to be worthy. I had to stop resisting who I really was and bring myself to the task of going back to my texts and allowing them to live. I decided right then and there that I was going to stop projecting my own dream of being all that I can be onto others: my children, their dad, and my clients. I was going to allow myself to do it myself.

This is what projection does. It keeps you in a place where you feel entitled to tell someone else what they should be doing differently, fooling yourself that if they take your advice and fix their issue, all will be well. It is a lie we tell ourselves, so we don't have to face our own denial, our fears, and vulnerabilities.

While you are projecting onto others, you cannot have your own breakthrough. You have to find what it is in yourself that you are only seeing on "the mirror." It's at the core of what is holding you back. Acknowledge yourself for your willingness to look at this issue from a new perspective.

The Ego Mask

One of the perhaps most difficult inner blocks to overcome is your particular "ego mask." Let me define ego since this word is being used widely and has gotten a bad reputation. The truth is, we all need a healthy ego. As defined by Britannica: "Ego, in psychoanalytic theory, is that portion of the human personality which is experienced as the "self" or "I" and is in contact with the external world through perception. It is said to be the part that remembers, evaluates, plans, and in other ways is responsive to and acts in the surrounding physical and social world." The ego is a person's sense of self-esteem. Synonyms include self-worth, self-respect, self-image, and self-confidence. Not to have an ego would mean that you would have no self-worth! So, let's clarify then that having a healthy ego is desirable, even necessary unless you want to be a doormat. It's the unhealthy ego that emerges from conscious and unconscious beliefs that are based in fear, that is undesirable, and that we wish to overcome.

Each one of us has fear-based beliefs. For example, you might have been severely scolded for failing at a particular subject at school when you were little, triggering your parents' anger and judgment—that they projected onto you, and you took on from them. This might have led you to believe that there is something wrong with you, that you are not good enough. This is a classic fear-based belief. To cope with the unresolved fear of not being good enough, and to make sure you are not the target of your parents' judgment again, you might have begun to deceive them when you got a bad grade, and you might have started to overemphasize areas in which you are doing well to compensate. This could have become your way of coping, of getting through your life. It might have become a pattern of deception and of showing off. It became your "ego mask." The problem is that you begin to identify with your mask, which is not who you really are.

Your ego mask hides your fear, and your shadow and makes it look desirable. For example, you might be driven to upgrade your home. This seems like a worthy goal. All the while, you're not realizing that you are driven by a fear of failure and worthlessness. If you were honest, you'd prefer to use the money you'll be spending on the renovation on making your dream come true, but you're not sure you'd succeed. You wouldn't want to face failure, so you avoid the debate and put it out of your mind. To keep the fear of failure at bay, it appeals to you to go after the "backup plan to happiness," the house renovation. You may even have a hunch that the work on the house is a distraction from what you're really here to do in your life, but you're too distracted to follow that thought. Another year goes by.

The payoff is that while you identify with your ego mask, you don't have to face your deepest fear or your most profound pain. The downside is that while operating from behind the ego mask, you are stuck in denial, and you can not be authentic, or emotionally free.

While still identified with your ego mask, the unhealthy ego's death feels synonymous with your own mortality. So essentially you could say that facing your ego mask feels like facing death. It takes a courageous person to make this step willingly. This is your "test." When you embrace your specific challenge, your breakthrough comes. This is when the pattern of denial suddenly ends.

> When we embrace our shadow, a miracle occurs.
> —Richard Rudd, *Gene Keys*

Perhaps the most extreme example of this phenomenon of being trapped in the unhealthy ego and in denial can be found in the inner circle of the Third Reich Nazis. These men were driven by a desire for megalomaniac power rooted in their own fear of failure and/or of worthlessness. Rather than facing their own shadow, they psychologically projected their lack of self-worth onto Jews, homosexuals and the disabled. Their core drive and ego fixation to rule the world was so powerful that it allowed them to stay in denial and ultimately lead to the Holocaust. The veneer of their delusion was so intact that it allowed them to believe the annihilation of six million Jews was in service to their country. The distortion of reality in these men in power allowed them to be indifferent to the horror they inflicted on the Jewish people. This is one extreme example of the ego mask firmly, and in this case, fanatically, in place. Any fanatical regime or dictatorship is based on a similar pattern of denial and projection.

> Evil is what you haven't accepted in yourself.
> —Richard Rudd, *Gene Keys*

We all have our "bullshit," our dysfunctions, our shadow to varying degrees. Our shadow is held in place by our denial of it. It is up to you to decide whether or not you can use the sobering humility that comes from facing your own shadow to snap out of your own denial. As soon as you meet your particular challenge, the denial suddenly ends. Two tools to help you discover your specific shadow and ego mask, so you can be streamlined and efficient about resolving the fear and pain that are keeping them in place, are the Enneagram and the Gene Keys.

The Enneagram is a system rooted in ancient wisdom that provides a map of how to understand yourself and others. The premise is that each of us takes on a personality trait, a mask, early on in life to help us survive. The Enneagram enables you to identify which particular cover you have identified with, so you can release it and remember that who you are beneath the mask is freedom. Once you discover the personality type you resonate with the most—through a questionnaire—you can distinguish your core avoidance mechanism and focus your inner work on clearing it.

The Gene Keys is a system, also rooted in ancient wisdom, that offers a gentle, contemplative path of self-inquiry that challenges, questions and enlightens you about your true role in life. It is a tool that enables you to pinpoint the shadow areas you have to face to set yourself free from within and overcome your ego fixation.

As humans, we have all the healthy and unhealthy ego traits in our spectrum. Admitting to them is a big step toward breaking free from unconsciously identifying with them.

Un-hook Yourself From Triggers

If you are triggered, the only way to free yourself from the grasp of that hook is by taking full emotional responsibility for what the trigger is bringing up in you.

STEP 8: Protocol to Unhook Yourself from Triggers

1. Recognize that you're triggered.
2. Stop reacting at once.
3. Flip your perspective from being mad at or irritated by the person or thing that is triggering you to being grateful for having your own "stuff" be pointed out to you.
4. Welcome the opportunity to identify what the trigger is pointing at in you.
5. Become still, breathe deeply, identify the emotion that is coming up. Let it flood over you. It might even feel like it will kill you. Trust it will only "kill" the unhealthy ego that is based on fear.
6. Contemplate: If the trigger is reflecting back to you something that you do, either to yourself or to others, what do you think it is? For example, you might be triggered by your child (or someone else) not respecting you. Then ask yourself how you are not respecting yourself (or others).
7. Open up and be as self-effacing as you possibly can.

8. Accept what you find out about yourself. Notice what you're noticing. Say to yourself: *Even though I am triggered, I love and approve of myself.* This creates the space for the fundamental shift to occur, and for you to have compassion, instead of anger or judgment for yourself as well as for the person you were triggered by.

Sooner or later, when you handle your triggers with this approach, it becomes apparent that we are all serving each other by pointing out where we have some work to do on ourselves. Once you accept that your own shadow is reflected back to you by others and that you're still lovable, it becomes easier to let go of attachment to the negative and to the positive and come into neutral.

> We are standing in a room full of mirrors.
>
> —Shai Magdish

The Power of Being Neutral

We are spiritual, vibrational beings having a physical, human experience. As such, we do not necessarily attract what we want, but always what we *are*, meaning what we are on a vibrational level. If you are frustrated because good hasn't come to you yet, or if you are head-over-heels excited because good is happening to you, you are emitting a vibration of either frustration about the perceived negative or attachment to the positive. Both attitudes can actually repel the good you are intending to attract.

To come into a place of neutrality, detach from complaining about the negative, as well as from craving the positive. This is how you situate yourself optimally to focus your manifesting skill. To arrive in a state of neutrality, you must first come to unconditional acceptance of both the negative and positive extremes which so often catch your attention and focus.

Neutrality Exercise

The things and people who trigger us the most point out our shadow. It is easier to see our own shadow reflected back to us by someone else than seeing it in ourselves. For this reason, we should really thank the people who trigger us for serving us in this way.

STEP 9:

1. Think of someone in your life who triggers you: your partner, your ex, your boss, your neighbor, your mother, your children, your siblings. Choose someone.
2. Notice how you feel about this person. What emotion does this person bring up in you? How does thinking about them make you feel?

3. Good. Now, as you think about the person, understand that how you are feeling towards them is your own feeling. As Shakespeare said, beauty is in the eye of the beholder. Consider that how you feel about the person who triggers you is entirely different to how someone else feels about them. Your feelings have more to do with you than with them. Own this. Whatever emotion this person brings up in you is your own feeling projected outside yourself. For instance, your boss who has control issues is reflecting back or triggering your own attitudes and feelings about power and control. Your competitive colleague triggers your own feelings about being competitive and reflects them back to you.

4. Throughout this week, whenever you think of this person or are triggered by them, remind yourself that the feelings are your own and that the person is serving you by making you become aware of these feeling. Rather than engaging in negative thoughts or stories about the person, accept that this trigger is something you need to accept within yourself. See if you can let go of any judgement directed at them and at yourself.

5. After one week of massaging your thoughts into a non-judgmental attitude, think of the person again. See how you feel about them now. Do you feel neutral about them now? Or still negative?

6. If you still feel negative about them, repeat step 4 and 5. The goal is to end up feeling neutral about the people who used to trigger you.

What do you do if anger or another strong negative emotion comes up and you find yourself projecting it onto someone? You take responsibility for it, remind yourself that it is an aspect of yourself, accept it, and by doing so melt it into neutrality.

> Your circumstances cannot be changed in the mirror.
>
> —Shai Magdish

Would you like help with this process? Connect with us at BlissKeys.com and choose your level of desired support.

Mind Joggers

STEP 10: If any of the questions below trigger you, journal about them here or in your notebook.

Are you seeing your gifts?

• Are you free to own your gifts? Are you disregarding magical aspects of yourself just because they come too easily?

_____

_____

_____

- Are you fixated and stuck on what you feel your success should look like, or how it should come about?

_____

_____

_____

Which limiting beliefs are still dominating your self-concept?

- Where do those beliefs come from? Whose voice, or point of view are they from?

_____

_____

_____

- What might be the unconscious psychological blueprint you took on from your parents? You only have to look at their life. What of the emotional quality of your parents' life mirror yours?

_____

_____

_____

- Have you ever run up against your inner blocks? Have you noticed a ceiling you can't seem to get past?

_____

_____

_____

Do you feel good about your heritage?

- Do you have ancestral or historical shame or guilt that you are carrying for "your people?" If so, would it lift your burden to release these emotions?

_____

_____

_____

Hakalau-ing Through The Terror Barrier

As you come closer to reaching your goal, or dream, the fear you encounter may increase. Fear shows up when you are at the edge of the life you know. Fear only confirms that you are pushing the envelope, which is good. If you're facing panic or terror, here is a protocol to get through it:

STEP 11:

1. Determine a tangible goal that you believe you can attain once you get to the other side of the terror barrier.
2. Create an image of your goal. Imagine yourself getting through the panic to get to this tangible goal.
3. Do the Hakalau exercise, as described at the beginning of the book in Module 1. Here is it again: Look at a spot on the horizon or wall twenty degrees above eye level—the height of your third eye. While gazing ahead, place your focus on the far right and the far left edge of your—now peripheral—vision. Stay in Hakalau for as long as you need, until the panic has subsided.

Bodywork

In addition to the emotional and cognitive clearing that we are focusing on in this module, we also have to clear our issues from our body. According to the Maori Healing tradition, our pain is stuck in our bones. It is essential to do bodywork, as well as Kundalini Yoga exercises to clear toxic cell memory and to strengthen your nervous system. This will help you to leave your limiting past behind and open into a more expansive, more authentic way of being alive.

Would you like info on bodywork and bodyworkers? Connect with us at BlissKeys. com and choose your level of desired support.

Module 8

Establish Your True You Feeling State

How quickly does your heart open after it has been shut down?

The Pain Of Opening Your Heart

This is the hardest chapter for me to write because when you are in your True You feeling state, your heart is wide open. When your heart is wide open, you feel your Love. When you feel your Love, you experience the pain of your loss. If this resonates, give a moment of silence in remembrance for whom or what you've lost.

STEP 1: If you are burdened by loss—recent or from long ago—allow yourself to mourn. Feel into the sadness, and release it. What have you lost? Whether it was a loved one, a part of yourself, or your dream, a pet, a friend, or innocence, the perceived loss of oneness, or belonging—let yourself feel it.

Have you given yourself time to mourn that loss? If you need more healing, find someone to help you through the process. Loss brings up different emotions. Let yourself go through the stages of the denial, the anger, the bargaining, the depression, and everything in-between until you come to the acceptance of it. Write about your journey through the feelings that come with loss here or in your notebook.

_____

_____

_____

_____

When you can let all the emotions surrounding the loss flow, re-creation can eventually begin again. If you would like someone to help you, find a Practitioner listed on the coaching hub at BlissKeys.com to assist you.

STEP 2: If you have experienced loss, how are you feeling about it now? Journal about it here or in your notebook.

_____

_____

_____

_____

When you think of a loss in your life, can you think of what you might have gained from that experience? What came after, that could not have happened if it hadn't been for the loss? Or maybe it is too early for that question. Put your thoughts to paper here or in your notebook.

_____

_____

_____

_____

STEP 3: If you are sensitive you may feel the pain of the world—the collective pain uniting humanity. Open your heart as wide as the world. Don't shut out the pain. By shutting out the pain, you're also shutting out the ecstasy. Stay wide open.

What does it feel like to open your heart as wide as the world? Contemplate as you write in a stream of consciousness—no self-censoring—just empty out.

_____

_____

_____

_____

When you come to recognize your Truth, the truth of your open heart, your fear-driven ego is no longer in the driver's seat. And this is what your ego wants to prevent. Your fear-driven ego—as opposed to your healthy ego—doesn't want you to wake up to the truth that at the level of your heart and in the depths of your own suffering you are equal with everyone else on this planet, and that the mind is only able to control a tiny aspect of your world. Your fear-driven ego thinks it should be able to control all of it, like the two-year-old inside of you that you once were—and still to some degree are—that is throwing tantrums when it learns that it is not in charge.

STEP 4: Because we are witnessing infantile leadership in our world, we have to ask ourselves—if we are being *triggered* by it—*what is this mirroring back to us?* In which way do you, do I, have "our inner two-year old" in the director's seat of our life? In what ways do you prefer to control life, instead of surrendering to the pain of your heart, and to the connection it brings? Just pose the question and, when you are inspired and insights come, write them down here or into your notebook.

_____

_____

_____

_____

You too, like the toddler self inside of you, have to surrender to the pain of not having ultimate control—it really sucks! There is no way around it. You have to surrender. This path is not through controlling or managing your emotions, but through welcoming and fully feeling them (as described in Module 4) until they have *burned up* and dissolved and you have landed in an emotion-less place of purely *being*, often referred to as Source.

Commit To Capturing The Energy Of Your Dream

You come into your True You feeling state when you decide to *defy* your lower consciousness frequencies such as grief, anger, guilt, shame, and *claim* your higher consciousness frequencies which include peace, love, and joy. Often this type of decision occurs in response to a blow of some kind—a situation in which you have to defend your dream and purpose against all odds.

The point of recovering your True You feeling state and then establishing it, is so that you can come back to it every day. It provides an emotional-spiritual anchor in your life. Your True You feeling state is also the *energetic magnet* for your dream.

There is a difference between pie-in-the-sky fairytale daydreaming, wishing on a star that is far out there and not realistic, but a lovely way to escape the reality of your life, and "confidently advancing in the direction of his dreams, endeavoring to live the life which he has imagined" (Thoreau). It comes back to commitment.

STEP 5: Recommit now by writing down and saying out loud: *I now confidently advance in the direction of my dreams, endeavoring to live the life which I have imagined.*

_____

_____

_____

_____

STEP 6: If you are afraid, or doubtful, remember a time in your past when you dared to show up for your dream, and transfer that courage onto now. Write about that time.

_____
_____
_____
_____

You will be rewarded.

> At the moment of commitment the entire universe conspires to assist you.
> —Johann Wolfgang von Goethe

> Once you make a decision, the universe conspires to make it happen.
> —Ralph Waldo Emerson

Permission

The decision to be your Highest Self and to live according to that standard of integrity entails no longer needing anyone else to give you permission to be magnificent. It means giving *yourself* permission to be all you came here for. It entails determination to fulfill your mission in life. This means, you have to have a strong sense of self and healthy boundaries, which I will talk about in Module 9.

STEP 7: Do you need to give yourself permission to be all you can be? If so, can you do that right now? Write down and speak out loud: *I give myself permission to be all that I came here to be.*

_____
_____
_____
_____

Do you feel you need permission from someone else? Write down your thoughts.

_____
_____
_____
_____

What will it take for you to get permission? Can you invite whomever you feel you need permission from to an *imaginary meeting place* and talk to them? What needs to be said? What do you need to get off your chest so you can feel empowered to give yourself permission to be *you*. What could never be said? Empty out here:

_____

_____

_____

_____

STEP 8: Are you still seeking approval from someone? Contemplate and write your thoughts in a stream of consciousness.

_____

_____

_____

_____

If you are still seeking approval from someone outside yourself, and you want to know if it is serving you or holding you back, determine how you feel—positive or negative, energized or depleted—after you have opened up to them. If the interaction leaves you feeling empty or drained, cut it. It's time to approve of yourself. Choose you.

As you know, the patterns you stay stuck in are the psychological wounds you have not yet healed. To come into your True You feeling state, you need to recognize if you are going back for more pain, unconsciously asking for "more whipping, please." A slight trait of masochism comes out in more people than you would think. There is an adrenalin rush when you get emotionally hurt. One of my clients, a medical doctor, told me self-inflicted emotional hurt may not be so different from self-inflicted physical cutting. This is when it gets tricky when you are chemically addicted to a feeling, which is also what's keeping you stuck. Becoming honest about what is happening is the first step to finally changing it. What do you still have to work through to be free to go on this journey? What do you need to clear to actively put your name to your dream and claim your True You feeling state? If you have more issues to remove, go back to Module 7 and clear your slate.

Do you have questions? Would you like guidance? Connect with us at BlissKeys. com and choose your level of desired support.

Trust Instead Of Manipulation

The goal is to establish your True You feeling state so you can capture the energy of your dream. Capturing the frequency of your dream is like being a landscape photographer on the look-out for that right light, that right angle to capture the beauty you see. To know the quality you are wishing to catch, you first have to know what it looks like and feels like. You first have to *be* it. The photographer cannot see the beauty if she is not looking for it. As Shakespeare said, beauty is in the eye of the beholder.

As the beholder of your dream, you have to come into your True You feeling state, so you have the right eyes to look through to capture the energy of your vision. It does not happen through manipulation, nor can it be willed by force. Capturing the energy of your dream can only occur by becoming synonymous with it. Manipulation only gets in the way of this.

STEP 9: To allow your dream to come to you, apply trust instead of force. Trust feels like letting go. Trust never occupies the same frequency as control. To feel trust, you have to let go of control. Breathe in a big breath of trust. Repeat as necessary.

The Universe doesn't respond well to you applying force or throwing a tantrum when you don't get what you want. We have to learn that we may not get it entirely in our own way. Your success may not look exactly the way you thought it would. You might be afraid of receiving less—but it's possible you might actually gain more. It might be beyond what you can imagine, beyond your wildest dreams. Let go of the need to control the outcome. You might find out that you are here to serve in a different way than you had in mind. Let it be. Be open to exchanging your fear-based ego drives with pure potentiality. Allow yourself to open your heart and to allow your destiny to reveal itself.

STEP 10: To practice letting go of control, stop cutting corners in traffic, quit getting in the way of the natural flow. Allow yourself to feel what it feels like when the universe's rhythm and your rhythm are in sync, and there is no need to manipulate. Practice acceptance as much as possible, without becoming a martyr.

STEP 11: As an exercise, imagine what it will feel like when you receive, not because you manipulate, strategize, or apply force, but because it is coming to you because you are allowing it to. Because you have become the *receptor* for it. And because you decided that it would.

STEP 12: Set your inner thermostat to *gratitude*. Write about everything you are grateful for, not just the positive things, but also the challenges, the lessons, the pain. Start your sentence with: *I am grateful for all that has brought me here…*_____

_____

_____

_____

_____

STEP 13: Reconnect with why you are pursuing your dream and why you have committed to being your True You in this life. Write about it. Start your sentence with: *I'm committed to being my True Self in this life because...*

_____

_____

_____

_____

STEP 14: Consider how your heart-born dream will benefit others. Write about it. Start your sentence with: *My dream will benefit others by...*

_____

_____

_____

_____

Healing Your Relationship To Money—The Blood Of The Planet

To be open to fully feeling your True You feeling state, you have to be open to receiving abundantly. Because receiving is associated with money, and money is likely to play a role in your endeavor to living the life you are imagining, let's talk about it here. What do you associate with *receiving*? What do you associate with *money*? It is essential that you clean up any unconscious beliefs around money, such as "money is the root of all evil," or "money corrupts." Theories that say that you can only have a spiritually rich life or a materially rich life, but not both, also have to be neutralized. The truth is you can have both—they are not mutually exclusive.

Recently, I had a revelation regarding money. It came from reading Barbara Walker's book *Money Is Love*. Walker offers a simple, hands-on approach to cleaning up your relationship with money on both a personal and a global scale by reconnecting to the *sacred origins of money*. She writes:

> From the earliest times, trade existed between tribes. The most traded item was food. Because food was sacred, the act of trading it was also sacred. In the Neolithic agrarian cultures circa 6,000 B.C.E., grains became the biggest trade item. The rituals surrounding the planting and harvesting of grain during the Neolithic era were the holiest times of the year, and the grain or corn gods were worshipped besides the Mother Goddess. The trading of the sacred grain was a sacred transaction. To cheat in a sacred transaction was to break faith with the

Divine, and to do this was not yet part of human consciousness. That would come later, as society became hierarchical. But in the early Neolithic, the sacred connection to the Mother Earth was still intact.

—Barbara Walker, *Money Is Love*

Attempting to teach the same point, I've witnessed Mary Morrissey standing on stage in front of fifteen hundred people, kissing a wad of money, and a feeling of unease going through the room.

STEP 15: Contemplate. What if money didn't have to be "dirty," "filthy," and "the root of evil?" What if you started thinking of money as being *sacred*, such as it was six thousand years ago, an extension of the Divine, handled with integrity? Write down your thoughts.

_____

_____

_____

_____

If the money that runs through your life is indeed part of the blood of the planet, how would you choose to think about it and relate to it? Would you still associate fear with it, lack, greed? Or would you be inclined to heal your attitude to it, to accept it as being an integral part of All That Is, of you?

STEP 16: If you didn't believe it was impossible what would it feel like having sufficient flow? Write about it. Start your sentence with: *If I didn't believe it was impossible, having abundant flow would feel…*

_____

_____

_____

_____

Imagine being comfortable with that reality. Let go of the fear around money—the anger, the sadness. Cleanse it by thinking every time you write a check, or charge your card: *Money is Love.*

Empty Your Cup

You can only capture the energy of your dream, and in the next module, *nurture your dream*, when you are empty enough for your vision to land in. How empty are you? If you are still "full of yourself," still grasping for the unhealthy ego's desire to "be someone," you are still filled with fear.

Emptying your inner cup means letting go of the "bullshit." Let go of all the fear-inspired fixations like envy and jealousy, like feeling not good enough, undeserving or unlovable. It means letting go of the root of your fear-based ego and of the unhealthy ego itself. Once and for all, identify your *poor me* story and commit to letting it go. Enough is enough. Be grateful for all that which brought you here, for the pain, for your humility. Accepting your most personally painful and perhaps humbling experiences—often labeled as failures—can serve you tremendously. Surrender to a higher version of you, one that doesn't have to be *right* anymore, but who chooses to be content instead.

If you haven't already, you may want to do a "No-Ego" Journey Process. It's an advanced process that will gently expose your fear-based drives, and free you of your unhealthy ego mask, so that you can be an empty vessel for your dream to land in.

Would you like to be guided through a "No-Ego" Process? Connect with us at BlissKeys.com and choose a Journey Practitioner to work with.

Denouncing The Victim

It's been established that how you relate to yourself has mostly to do with your conscious and unconscious thoughts about yourself and about life. Get into the habit of checking in and seeing how you are feeling. Is your heart open? Or are you caught up in turmoil, jealousies or envy? Is there bitterness, or suspicion? Are you feeling like the victim?

In this module there is no more room for the victim in you, or for you to identify with being the victim—which can come in many disguises. All the benefits and secondary gains you get from being in a state of "life happening *to* you" have to be cleared. If they haven't yet, go back to Clear Your Slate in Module 7, and chisel away a bit more. It's the real work we all have to do to have true inner peace. You don't really get a choice. There is no way around it—only through it. This is the time to become definite about taking the step to transform your role in your life, once and for all.

Pass Through Your Own Suffering

On our journey of self-discovery, self-growth, and self-actualization, we move in an upward spiral. We circle around the same issues, again and again, seeing them from an ever-evolving perspective, with ever-deeper understanding. Now that you are fine-tuning your feeling state to your True You, there can't be any more finger-pointing or blame. "Evil is everything you haven't accepted," writes Richard Rudd, author of *The Gene Keys,* the guide to addressing your specific fear-based ego patterns. Feel free to replace the word *evil* with *shadow*. What Rudd is referring to is what American psychologist Milton Eriksson meant when he said that we project our own shadow onto others, often the people we are closest to. It is easier to see your shadow anywhere but in yourself. Instead of blame, *love the shadow away*. Move beyond it. Become more significant than your shadow by accepting that it is a part of you and that you are a part of it.

The Hawaiian distant healing practice of Ho'Oponopono works by the practitioner taking full emotional responsibility for the negative issue he witnesses in the person he's working on and then restoring sacred, spiritual union between the person and their Higher Self through forgiveness. You don't have to become a practitioner of Ho'Oponopono and heal others, but you will need to heal, or at least neutralize, your own issues when they are being reflected back to you by someone else, triggering you to reach for blame. Why? Because blame and your True You feeling state are on different vibrational frequencies, and cannot co-exist. You have to reach beyond pointing the finger to be in your True You feeling state.

Deciding to establish your True You feeling state and to leave the old paradigm behind requires an emotional breakthrough. Through breaking down emotionally, defense patterns can be revealed. The pain comes out, and the wound can be healed. True emotional discovery involves a crisis. Your life will offer you opportunities. How you respond determines how deeply you let the transformation occur. Journeywork can be a facilitator for this transformation. By surrendering to feeling your emotions fully, you descend deeply into unconscious waters, further than conscious memory can go. You remember through your being, not through your mind. You remember through a feeling. You do that by breathing deeply into your emotions, and by having unconditional positive regard for yourself in the process (see Module 4).

It is the intelligence of Love that witnesses and drives your transformation, that teaches you how to live life with all its challenges with an open heart. Be open to feeling your heart-core woundedness, the core of what makes you human. Pass through your own suffering. Do it with style, or do it without, like it or not, just do it. This is you reaching the Source. You transcend your own suffering by breathing into it, physically, literally.

Notice your perceived emotional needs, and realize that you have the choice to let go of your attachment to them. As you continue to let go of your devotion to the old ways, you establish new ways of doing things and relating to life.

Strip your emotions of the attached story, and you will see your feelings are just energy. Allow this energy to be free from the story, free from meaning. If anything, imagine it being life force, sacred power and be present to it when it moves through you. Honor it by breathing deeply and releasing your fear-based ego needs, your triggers, every chance you get, so you can be a good host for this sacred life energy to move through and for your dream to land in. Become a fertile ground for your clear intention to be planted in.

Let It Be Physical

STEP 17: Start to get physical. Feel your body. If you are not exercising regularly, then start now to stretch and tone your muscles with easy-to-do exercises. Start in your own room if need be. Get a yoga mat if you don't have one, and you want to upgrade your in-home exercise station.

If you have a yoga regimen already, then let yourself be physical in a new, less structured way. Feel your emotions, as much as your muscles, as you lean into the stretch that comes naturally. Allow feelings to come up. Breathe into the stretch. Meet the discomfort or pain with your awareness and comforting thoughts. Calm your mind. If that's hard, just practice Hakalau.

Give, give, give to yourself, funnel your energy towards yourself. Allow whatever negative or positive emotion is there to be felt in its pure form. Feel just the emotion, not the story. Disengage from the story. Stop negotiating in your mind. Stop defending yourself. Stop the maneuvering, the fear-based strategizing. Finish with this type of behavior. Illuminate it as fear-based, accept it is driven by your unhealthy ego. Understand that this path can not, by definition, lead you to your promised land. Nip it in the bud and go back into Hakalau. Hakalau is your declaration to make a 180-degree turn, away from this self-narcotizing behavior of staying stuck in limbo land. Be done with it. Hakalau yourself into a better equipped nervous system to be the person you are meant to be. You have some physical, neurological work to do. You have to reprogram and strengthen your nervous system to allow such ease into your life—so much joy, so much expansion, and so much abundance.

Get Good With Change

Once you acclimatize to facing your own shadow, you may begin to feel better in your skin. Maybe it is subtle, and you only notice that you are not reacting anymore to specific incidents that, in the past, would have triggered you. You're staying equanimous more. Let it happen, let it in. Let yourself feel the expansion of allowing change to occur.

STEP 18: To accelerate your evolution consciously welcome the *temporary chaos* that comes from the inner changes you are making. Plant moments of temporary confusion into your day. Deliberately misplace your house keys, or change one of your routines. If you get out of bed a certain way in the morning, do it differently. Put your shoes on with the other foot first. Prepare yourself to be comfortable with change.

How can we help you? Connect with us at BlissKeys.com. Send us your questions and comments.

MODULE 9

NURTURE YOUR DREAM

Give your attention to what you wish to create. Be passionate about your dream.

To *nurture* means to care for and encourage the growth or development of something. For your dream life to grow and develop, you need to care for it and support it as if you were nurturing a child.

STEP 1: What does that look like practically? What are ways that you can nurture the life you are endeavoring to live? Brainstorm on this. Start your sentence with: *Ways that I can nurture the life I am endeavoring to live, are...*

_____

_____

_____

_____

Nurture the ideas and thoughts that arise by following them through to the end. Listen to your dream, it will tell you what it needs from you, as well as what it requires you to avoid doing so that you and your goal can develop into their full potential.

Stay Tuned To Your Heartfelt Desire

Your greatest ally in the dream-weaving process is the passion you have to create what it is that you are envisioning. Stay tuned to your True You feeling state. Bring it into your body.

STEP 2: Walk like you're already living your dream. Release the stagnant energy by moving your hips. Stay flexible and juicy.

At the Goddess Returns Retreat with Maori Master healer Atarangi Muru, Ata enticed us twenty female participants to "essence." She used the word as a verb, asking us to exude our spirit, our nature as we walk down the street and down the supermarket aisles.

Your mind will try to talk you out of your dream. It will come up with a thousand fear-based reasons why it is impossible for it to come true, or too dangerous, or too embarrassing.

STEP 3: Make sure you always have one good reason to stay focused on your dream. What is your reason—your real reason—for why you have to give your dream a shot? Start with the words: *The real reason I am giving my dream a shot is because...*

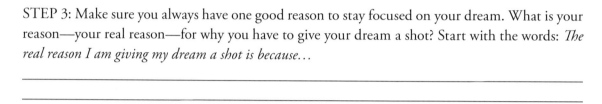

If you get caught up in your mind, and it's limiting beliefs about what is and what isn't possible, you can get sucked into a downward spiral and lose sight of your dream. However, by staying tuned to your True You feeling state you protect your vision from your own doubts. Envelop it in a protective shield.

Make a practice out of feeling your dream as if it were already here. Even if you have a long way to go to bring it to fruition—even if you do not know yet how you will come up with the resources, the contacts, the know-how to make it happen—stay firm in your True You feeling state. If doubts come in, believe that because you have a dream, a dream that is coming from the depths of your heart, it is yours to create in this life. Protect this notion, and strengthen it by feeling deeply into the core of the life you are endeavoring to live. The more you practice this, the more your confidence will grow and the easier it will be to shrug off notions of doubt before they pull you and your spirit down.

STEP 4: If doubts or self-depreciation persist, or if you get a good look at your own shadow behavior, practice self-acceptance by saying to yourself: *What if I had to be exactly this way, including this shadow, to have the experiences and awarenesses to evolve into my highest potential?* By having a positive attitude towards your own shadow, you actively integrate it into your Self. This way it doesn't have to act out anymore to gain your attention.

STEP 5: Do not lend your ear to naysayers, or people who doubt you, or cause you to question yourself. Become good at intuiting whom you can and cannot share your dream with. Nurture your idea by only telling people who will encourage you instead of pull you down.

Setting Boundaries —Saying No To Emotional Vampires

You have to get exceptionally good at setting healthy boundaries and protecting your dream from people whose acknowledgment you crave. Sometimes such people suck your energy and make you doubt yourself. Needing acceptance is a weakness that usually comes from a part of you that feels like it hasn't been loved or seen for who you really are. However, as long as you are still seeking acknowledgment from outside yourself, you may project your need onto people who are not capable of seeing your full potential, or who are unconsciously threatened by you, or who want to hold you back.

You have to become proficient at distinguishing people who will support your dream from people who are energy vampires. When you notice the person you are sharing your idea with is sucking your energy, stop sharing your vision! I've started sentences, then realized I'm talking to a naysayer, and changed the sentence midway, as not to invite their energy in.

A friend of mine has an unhealthy pattern of falling in love with men who end up taking her for granted. Several months ago, she came to me complaining about it. Fed up with her reoccurring pattern, she asked why she is doing it. I know from what she has told me about her childhood that she felt unseen as a child. If her parents did not reciprocate the love she gave them as a child in a way that she needed them to, she might have learned to devalue herself. Out of a wish to still be loved by her parents, she may have started projecting this need onto others—giving her time, love, energy, attention and creativity to people who are not returning it to her the way she needs it—making herself re-live the same pain again and again. The hope that "they will one day see her for who she really is" may have driven her to hold onto this type of behavior and to project it onto one boyfriend after the next.

Upon seeing her pattern, she was finally able to do the inner work necessary to let it go. As a result, her self-respect went up, and for the first time, she now has a relationship in which she feels seen. She first had to see and respect herself, before she could attract someone who would see and recognize her for the beautiful, bright and funny person she truly is.

If this or a similar scenario resonates with you, you will benefit greatly by exploring why you engage in giving your love, energy, and hope to someone who is unable to return it to you the way you need it. Your own reason for this self-inflicted pain lies hidden in your unconscious. The Belief Change Exercise in Module 7 will help you uncover it. Then, do the Boundary Exercises below to stop leaking your energy to people who are unable to reciprocate in ways that meet your needs.

Boundary Exercise

STEP 6: Find a private place where you will be uninterrupted for at least five minutes.

1. Identify who you are leaking your energy to.
2. Identify if you are trying to impress them.

3. Then, at an *imaginary meeting place—as if* they were there with you—tell them to leave you alone, to get out of your energetic field. Be strong. Shout at them if you feel like it. Really mean it.

4. Check with yourself if you are willing to let that behavior go. Are you ready to draw a healthy boundary around yourself?

5. If yes, imagine the person whose approval/love/recognition you want, sitting eight feet in front of you. Now draw an '8' or infinity symbol, around yourself and this person, with the point where the lines cross in between you.

6. Follow the infinity symbol with your inner eye, and imagine seeing the spot where the lines cross, light up in blue.

7. Imagine the love, acknowledgment or respect that you have been trying to get from the person who is NOT returning it to you, and direct it onto yourself.

8. Do this exercise regularly, until you feel healthily detached from the person in question.

Nurturing Means Staying Close To

In the Maori culture, I was told, the women cooking the food will not leave the stove while cooking. They will stay close to the food, infusing it with their loving energy. I don't know if you have ever tasted a meal prepared with this consciousness. I have, and you can literally feel and taste the love in the food. To love and to nurture means to stay present with what it is that you are cultivating. The same goes for your dream. Stay current with it, watch over it. Know how it's doing. Infuse your love and care into it every moment of the day. Do it with your heart, by feeling a connection with it. Know that it is up to you to keep it alive, to give it the environment to thrive in. Your dream needs you. You are its creator. So you have to be present with it to make it all it can be.

STEP 7: To make this practical, capture the energy of your dream in a short version of your vision statement and place it somewhere where you will see it daily. If you are a visual person, find or draw a picture that encapsulates your dream's essence and makes you think of living it. If you are auditory, and you learn best by hearing, find music or a mantra that reminds you of your dream and listen to it, hum it. If you are kinesthetic and you respond to physical activities, find actions that remind you of the life you are endeavoring to live. It could be putting on a song and dancing to it. It could be taking a bubble bath, and using a lotion your True You loves. Be creative and find ways that link you to the life you are envisioning.

Be Impeccable With Your Word

To nurture your dream also means that you have to protect it from your own harmful speech. We know from quantum physics and metaphysics that thoughts direct energy and energy follows thought.

Your mind thinks in pictures and whatever you speak about is what your mind will make pictures of, and whatever you make pictures of in your mind is what you actively bring into your life. Your brain doesn't differentiate whether or not you want what you are speaking about. All that counts is the pictures that your thoughts and your words are creating. If you make the statement that you *do not* want to be broke, for instance, all that your mind sees is a picture of you being broke.

STEP 8: It is essential to create a picture of what it is that you *do* want. So, if you're going to be financially abundant in your life, talk about *having* money, instead of not wanting debt. Choose words that create the picture of what it is that you do want.

The more passionate you are about what you are saying, the more energy you are giving towards its manifestation. So, it is of utmost importance that you be impeccable with your word, and that you avoid passionately ranting or raving about all the terrible things you don't want to happen.

To illustrate, here is an example from one of my clients. At the beginning of her recent coaching call, she expressed her upset about her financial goal not having manifested yet. Her words were negative, negating even the positive results she has had so far. Her attitude had blame in it, blaming her circumstances. I asked her what she had been actively doing, what her practice had been this last week regarding her inner work. She revealed that she has actually been doing really well, creatively moving forward, and then mentioned three positive developments—including one in which she is saving thousands of dollars on a marketing deal. I remind her to pay more attention to the positive events and take full responsibility for her thinking and her feeling, including her attitude, and the pictures she is creating in her mind. I remind her that she has to quit being the victim. Any finger pointing is going to stand in her way of being fully empowered. In particular, she has to be diligent about the words she uses to describe her situation.

Especially when you are worked up, afraid of not having enough money in the bank, for instance, and you couple this nervous energy with emotionally charged stories of lament, you are only reinforcing your current undesirable circumstances. If you spot yourself doing something similar, stop and go into self-inquiry. Go back to Module 7 and find out what your deep unconscious beliefs and definitions are that are still creating the old limiting circumstances. Journal about the areas of your life that are still not lining up, not to dwell on the negative, but to purify your well by pumping out the sluggishness. Practice being impeccable with your word. Eliminate talking about what it is that you *don't* want, and choose to stay focused on what it is that you *do* want.

Partners In Believing

Success doesn't come in isolation. You don't have to nurture your dream alone. In fact, each of you needs a *partner in believing*—someone who can hold the space for you to birth your true self.

STEP 9: Find someone who believes in you—whom you trust, who encourages you to move beyond your comfort zone, and who will hold you to your full potential. The coaching hub at BlissKeys.com and my one-on-one program is an excellent partner in believing. The one-on-one work I do with my clients is all about the space I hold for them so they can be open, vulnerable and authentic—so they can shed all that which is not their true self and focus on that which is. When their old negative patterns of doubt or feelings of being undeserving pull them down, I pull them back up, reminding them of their potential. I encourage and inspire them to continue nurturing their dream. You need a safe space to birth your true self. It can not happen otherwise. The Bliss Keys coaching hub at BlissKeys.com provides such a space for you.

Prayer

Prayer is one of the most powerful ways of being in a close intimate relationship with your dream. If the word *prayer* brings up resistance in you—if you are uncomfortable with it, or it feels foreign—exchange the word *prayer* with *intention*. When you pray, you open up the channel between you and your higher self. The depth and intensity of your prayer or intention impact the results you will have.

STEP 10: Could you allow your heart to open and to feel deeply into your intention? Give yourself the space to ask for what you would love. Are you open to accepting it being given? Can you receive the blessing? Do you feel deserving of it?

You don't need a reason for your dream. That you have it is reason enough to go after it. What does your heart truly desire? What is most important to you? Pray for it. Passionately. Set your intention. Start with the feeling of gratitude for it already being given. Write your prayer or intention down.

_____

_____

_____

Would you like help with these exercises? Do you have questions or comments? Connect with us at BlissKeys.com and choose your level of desired support.

MODULE 10

CREATE THE LIFE THAT MATCHES YOUR TRUE SELF

Let go of trying to make it happen. Accept it as already being here.

Cyclic Energy

To deliberately co-create your life, it is helpful to identify the cyclic energy that is influencing you at any given moment. As mentioned at the beginning in Agreements, everything in life boils down to *energy*. And just as the tides of the ocean are caused by the gravitational pull of the moon and the sun, you too are influenced by the cyclic force moving in and out of your experience.

To make the most out of these cyclic energies, it helps to get good at knowing which one is moving through you, and then adjust yourself to it so you can utilize it to your advantage. By approaching your co-creating and dream weaving quest in this way, you may be surprised that you have to do a lot less legwork than you may think. A lot of the *doing* that needs to happen is internal, passive, is merely *being*. And when you do take action, it is inspired action you take. A lot of the pushing and effort-ing is entirely ineffective and actually slows down the process. I just had one of my clients tell me she sacrificed a whole summer, spending no time with her children, all because she was anxious to get her house on the market. Her mission came to a screeching halt, right when the house looked perfect, and the photos for the listing were scheduled. The septic tank needed attention, and the entire front yard was torn up. There is a better, more sustainable way than to exhaust yourself. There is a more harmonious way.

Imagine the ubiquitous yin-yang symbol. For those of you who are not familiar with it, the yin-yang symbol is a circle divided by an S-shaped line into dark and light segments, representing yin and yang, each containing a seed of the other. Yin, the dark swirl, is associated with shadows, the feminine principle—intuition, receptivity, and gestation. Yang, the light swirl, represents brightness, the masculine principle—passion, logic, growth, and inspired action. In Chinese philosophy, yin and yang describe how seemingly opposite or contrary forces may actually be complementary, interconnected, and interdependent in the natural world. They give rise to each other as they interrelate to one another. Both forces are a part of this dualistic world we live in—both are a part of you, and both need to be applied in the creation of your dream.

STEP 1: How do you know which cyclic energy you are in? Yin or yang? Just ask yourself: *Do I feel more like being or acting?* Check in with your body. Become still enough so you can distinguish the difference. Breathe deeply to calm yourself down so you can evaluate where you're at.

If your circumstances are forcing you to slow down, if your plans are not panning out, if you are hitting roadblocks, take a step back. If you find yourself pushing towards your goal, but you're not feeling inspired, then stop. It may just be that you are pushing ahead, in yang energy, and that your cycle needs you to be in yin, in merely *being* mode.

If life is giving you signals—electronics acting up used to be a common one for me—just disengage for a moment. Switch focus. Breathe, be, relax. Get up, move, stretch, or go for a walk. Tune into your body and feel what it wants, needs, or currently harmonizes with. Instead of pushing ahead, reexamine and reevaluate where you are at. Tune into your breathing. You may want to use the time to reassess your vision statement. Sometimes it can be the time to restore, to sort, to set things right. When sailors can't go to sea, they mend their nets. Reflect and yield. Once you have released the need to push on, and have taken a moment to breathe—to be—you may soon find yourself aligned again with yang mode. Nourished by having replenished in yin mode, you're once again inspired to approach your goal from a more logical, passionate and purposeful perspective.

STEP 2: To create your dream, commit or recommit yourself now to a daily practice. This can include Kundalini Yoga, Hakalau, journaling, communion with nature, prayer or intention setting, and deep breathing.

My minimum daily practice consists of ten minutes of Kundalini in the morning and Hakalau whenever I need it, i.e., when I am in a funk or triggered. It also includes self-inquiry, either through contemplation or through journaling whenever required. It is not so much *time* you need for this work, it is a *dedication* to always come back to your center. Whatever it takes. If that means staying off of Facebook for a day, a week, or longer, so be it. If it means filling the creative well with binge watching a show, and enjoying that thoroughly, so be it.

It also means being smart about things. Alcohol is a depressant, for instance. So if you are working on becoming stronger by raising your energy, then having a drink every night is not going to help that. Don't sabotage yourself. Do what makes sense, at your own pace. The stronger you become in your daily practice, the easier it will be for you to tune into your own energy and know which part of the cycle you're in. When it is time for intuitive, under the surface work, do it. When it is time to apply logical, purposeful action, do it.

STEP 3: Practice it now: Ask yourself what your body needs. Does it need to rest? Sleep? Does it need to calm down, to center itself? Does your mind need to get still? Or, are you ready to receive inspiration? Are you in intuitive daydreaming mode? Are you in creative visualization mode? If so, lean into it. If you feel like insight is about to stream in, get pen and paper and start taking notes. Are you in brainstorming mode? If so, write all your thoughts and ideas down. Do not edit any of them out. Circle those that have the most "pull." Any hunches? Trust them.

Are you in logical action mode? Can you feel that you have to do something? Then do it. Take inspired action. Always make sure that your inspired action is in service of your purposeful goal. And that your purposeful goal is in service to your heart's desire.

If you are unable to determine which cyclic energy is moving in and out of your experience, check to see if you feel scattered or unfocused, possibly by having too many things on your plate. If this is the case, you may want to narrow it down and become more single-minded.

Emotion Of Desire

STEP 4: Once you have a sense of which cyclic energy is moving in or out of your experience, tune into your heart-born—as opposed to fear-born—desire. Let yourself feel it fully.

Focus your thought. Clarify your personal vision. What is one thing that when it eventuates indicates your dream has manifested? Find that one picture in your mind, in your inner eye. Now write it down. The wording is essential.

_____

_____

_____

For example, if you are working on improving your relationship, state your goal from the perspective of already having achieved that, as opposed to still having to get there. *I am enjoying my wonderful relationship.* Not: *I am working on having a better relationship.*

Or, if your goal is financial comfort, state your purpose as: *I have more than enough money in the bank.* Not: *I am making more money.*

The choice of words is important because if you are focused on *still getting there*, you will stay stuck in a *never-ending loop of getting there*, which will be exhausting and ineffective. If you state your goal as already having ensued, however, and you see and feel yourself already reaping the benefits, you will be surprised to find yourself *in* your preferred reality.

Let's say your goal is to live your life purpose. If you say, however, that your goal is to *find* your life purpose, as opposed to *living it*, your life is going to become a never-ending journey of having reason to find your life purpose. Welcome to a labyrinthian search. Could you instead focus on already living your life purpose?

STEP 5: Fine-tune the words you choose and become aware of the scenario that the words create for you in your mind. So if your dream is to thrive while living your life purpose, picture that. Check your sentence above and see if it's worded as *getting there* or *already being there*. The words you use, program your mind and will deliver very different life experiences for you. Experience the end result you desire right now emotionally. Don't focus on having to change your reality, because if you do, you will experience a reality that needs to be changed. Equally don't focus on having to change your self, because if you do, you will experience a self that needs to be changed. Instead, focus on already being the one you want to be, your True Self. Walk and talk like her/him right now.

> One of the things that may be surprising is that when you intend to live your life purpose, living your life's purpose is going to be the result that will be in your experience.
>
> —Shai Magdish

Top-Down-Living

In Module 3, I mentioned the term *Top-Down-Living*. Top-Down-Living means that you first reach your source—the inner state of pure potentiality, healthy detachment and pure being-ness—and then do all of your brainstorming, visualization and taking inspired action from there.

Top-Down-Living means that you actively follow Thoreau's formula, "endeavoring to live the life you are imagining." Wake up in the morning as the person you endeavor being. Think like the person you are in the life you are imagining. Dress like this person as best you can with your current means. Talk, breathe, walk, sit like the person you're becoming. Read the books this ultimate version of you would be reading. You are allowing your True You to be you.

Top-Down-Living means that you live your life from a feeling place of having already arrived where you want to be. It says you live your life in connection with your desire, your yearning, and allow it to drive you toward your destiny.

STEP 6: To practice this on a daily basis, get into the habit of going into the peripheral vision exercise, Hakalau—mentioned in Agreements, in Module 6 and 7—the moment you start reacting to a trigger. This is a fast way to center yourself. Or, if you prefer and you are experienced in the emotional release work—feel deeply into any negative emotion the moment it arises until you drop through it into source and neutrality. Then just decide what you would *prefer,* picture your preference having manifested and smile.

Paving The Way With Your Thoughts

When you create something, you first *think* about it. If you strip the creative process down to its bones, you could say that it consists of two significant steps: 1.) You decide what you are going to do. 2.) You do it.

Imagine a simple creative act, such as drinking a glass of water. Once you have decided that you are going to drink, what happens? You automatically take the glass, you bring it to your mouth, and you drink. Your toddler-self learned this action through observation and practice. When you do the act of drinking a glass of water, you don't worry about it not working. You don't procrastinate because you feel unworthy, and you're not afraid of what might happen once you have achieved it. You simply do it. This is the process of creation. You make the decision, and then you let it happen. You do it automatically. You don't overthink it and come up with reasons why it can't be done, or why it isn't safe, you just do it.

If it is this simple to create something, then why isn't it easier to create harmony and abundance in all areas of life? It's because, to merely decide and do something, you have to *believe* that you can, and feel hopeful of it happening. You have to see it in your mind so that you can emulate it. The toddler would not have been able to manage the creative act of drinking water by merely deciding to, had he not first learned how to do it by observing it.

STEP 7: How do you create a future that you haven't seen modeled? You do it by creating this future in your mind. You have to *imagine it* and *feel* what it will feel like when the future you envisioned is here and has become your new normal.

Deliberate Co-Creation

STEP 8: To let this be as simple as it can be, first determine the phase of your cyclic energy.

Yin Mode

1. When you are in yin—being—mode, remind yourself that you are a creator, deserving of what you are asking for.
2. Remind yourself that your manifesting power is stronger than your circumstances.
3. Ask for what you desire, from the perspective of already having been given it.

4. Be patient and grateful for it making its way to you. Let go of the desperate need for it, by feeling as if it is already here. Trust that the physical manifestation of it will come.

5. Envision it coming. Expect it to happen. Feel grateful for it has arrived.

6. Stop any doubt or mind-wandering with the Hakalau exercise.

7. Be open to receiving.

8. Notice the blessings you already have and give thanks for them. Bless all you have, and everything that brought you here.

Yang Mode

1. When you are in yang—inspired action—mode, focus your thoughts on your goal and brainstorm ideas for inspired action.

2. Write all your ideas down.

3. Circle the ideas that stand out and have the most energy.

4. Be aware of hunches and follow them at once.

5. Take inspired action.

6. You reap what you sow: Activate the flow of abundance by "stoking the fire, and by putting wood on the fire." Give, give—receive. Give, give—receive. If you're intending to gain more clients, for example, first give of your services—a free sample, a complimentary introductory session. Get the fire going. Plant the seeds. Then open to receive.

7. Note: How you put it out there is how it comes back to you. If you are asking for a fantastic relationship, wish for others to be in fulfilling relationships. If you want to be financially abundant, desire for others to have sufficient flow. When you pay for your groceries, imagine the store making a good profit. Grant others what you wish for yourself.

Troubleshooting: Transferring Success-Consciousness To Areas In Need

1. If you are having trouble succeeding at your goal, find one area that is working well in your life—where success comes easily. Notice how you feel about that area of life. Notice your beliefs about it. Then transfer that ease and positive expectation onto the areas of life that you have issues with.

2. Beware of self-sabotage: In case you notice any beliefs that say *you can't*, change them into positive beliefs/truths through a Belief Change Process (Module 7).

Using Visualization

1. When you think about something that you know for sure, such as the sun rising tomorrow morning, where does the picture of this particular incident appear in your body? Where

do you sense it? Some experience this certainty close to their brain, some in their heart. Locate this area in your body or energetic field. Then place an image of the attainment of your dream in that same spot.

2. Make a future timeline of your dream having eventuated. Imagine your life one year from now, two years from now, three years from now. What is your life like? In your mind, place your success in your future timeline. If any resistance or disbelief show up, go back to Module 7 and clear your slate with the Belief Change Exercise. If you need help, choose your level of support at the BlissKeys.com coaching hub.

3. Let's say your goal is to move into another home. Look at a piece of furniture that you'll take with you and imagine it in the new house. Alternatively, as you walk through your current home, imagine walking through your new home and feel how good that feels.

Following Your Intuition

Are you relying on your own intuition in your life choices? Or are you seeking answers from someone outside yourself? Are you other-directed, or self-directed? If other-directed, how do you feel about that? Is it your choice to be other-directed, or does it happen by default? Do you have a role model of someone, your gender, who is self-directed? What do you like about them? Journal about that.

_____

_____

_____

Quantum-Leaping

1. Remind yourself of who you are: a child of this creative, intelligent universe.
2. Determine what you are quantum leaping into. What is a sign that you have arrived? What is your actual definable goal?
3. Think of how much you are willing and comfortable to receive? How much do you feel comfortable being responsible for?
4. Feel how it will feel when it has ensued. Make sure it is for the highest and best for all involved and place your dream in service of a higher good.
5. Brainstorm. Open your mind to ways to receive information that will lead you to your goal. What is the one next thing you have to do? Follow hunches. Use inspired action.
6. Is there doubt? No worries. Is there fear? No problem. Starve them. If doubt or fear persists, find out what the benefit is of holding on to them. (Belief Change Exercise, Module 7.)

7. Emotions. Are a lot of emotions coming up? Remember, the feeling is not you. Emotion is just energy in motion. The moment you have a sad or negative definition attached to the sentiment, it's now become more than energy in motion, it's become a story. The more *meaning* you give it, the more you'll identify with it. Stop giving the feeling meaning. Just feel the energy in it. Let it flow through you. Release it. Reach your Source.

8. Forgiveness. Cut energetic ties. Make peace inside so you can move on.

9. Flow state. Give yourself permission to free yourself from your limiting environment and in-the-box expectations. Follow your own passion, your impulse, your yearning. What do you need so you can perform at your best?

10. What action step have you been avoiding? Why are you avoiding it? What is the worst that could happen? What is the best that could happen?

11. Experience your dream through all your senses. Act as if it's already here.

12. Welcome temporary confusion.

13. Get rid of clutter. Prepare the space for your dream life.

You being you with
gratitude and clarity of intention
is bound to create what you are envisioning and sensing.

Would you like more information and hands-on-guidance on how to use the deliberate manifestation techniques? Connect with us at BlissKeys.com and choose your level of desired support.

MODULE 11

EXPAND YOUR REACH

Tell Your Story

One of the most powerful ways to expand your reach and touch others is to tell your story. It doesn't have to be by writing a book. It may be in relating to others and through the anecdotes you share. Stories have been told throughout time. They help us understand ourselves, each other, and life. Stories help us heal—especially ones that are derived from going on a self-exploration journey such as the one you're on.

Throughout this coaching program, you have gained a deep understanding of yourself. You have been, and perhaps still are, on your own inner journey of liberation from identities you thought were you, and the limitations you felt were real. You have been healing your issues at their emotional root cause. The ripple effect of your work has the potential to touch many others. True healing and transformation happen when you fully accept yourself as you are—by getting to know yourself inside and out—your positive and negative attributes, and by recognizing that all of it is a part of you.

STEP 1: The next step is to become fully conscious of your own transformation and to touch others by being an example, inspiring them to live their highest potential. How you do this, and the form it takes is entirely up to you. It will however, have an element of *story* in it.

If you have a desire to excavate the seeds of your personal journey and to uncover your unique story of awakening, you can utilize this program to create a role for yourself or to tell your story in a book, script or series. Coming to terms with your own life issues gives you deep insight into the human condition and deepens your creative work.

If you are an entrepreneur, you can weave your wealth of insight into your unique life story in your blog posts, videos, and other marketing tools. Remember facts tell, but stories sell.

Years ago I studied film directing and script writing. I wrote several scripts, but I lacked deep insight into my self, and the scripts I wrote became challenging to finish. The character arcs and the psychological through-lines were unclear to me. After years of doing mind-body healing and laser-coaching, I know how to access the authentic, juicy stuff of life. I have found how to go deeply into my own inner truth, my unconscious—my uncensored self. Now, I have a never-ending well of story material. If you have the desire to do that yourself, I can guide you to excavate the seeds of your own story and empower you to tell your own.

Would you like more information on how to use this method to write your own soul-directed story or role? Connect with us at <u>BlissKeys.com</u>. Send us your questions and comments.

Live Your Purpose

Collective harmony is achieved through individual freedom and trust in the self- organizing intelligence that emerges from this freedom.

—Richard Rudd, *Gene Keys*

I believe that the individual freedom that Richard Rudd talks about in the quote above occurs when people live their life purpose. The happiness and inner peace from living your purpose have ripple effects that positively affect the collective. You are the only one who can honestly know what it is that you are here to do in your life, what your gift is, your purpose, your calling. It is yours to find and yours to live. When I did my Life Purpose Process in 2007, in the last module of the intense one-year training of the Journey Practitioner Program, what I got was not a job description—*your purpose is to be an actress and play the role of...*, or *your mission is to be a mother of two...*, not even *your role is to be a life coach and write self-help books.* What I got was a feeling, a remembering of a state of being, an intrinsic knowing of what I am here for. The words that came to me in the process were *You're here to shine and to remind.* When I tuned into who I was meant to remind, and of what, I got *As many people as possible, of the love that is at the core of each and every one of you.* At its heart, your purpose is more a state of being, than an action. However, by becoming synonymous with your purpose, you will see it become your life, your activities, your message.

To shine, I had to come out from behind the shadow. That has been my journey, as depicted in my coaching memoir, *Breaking Out Gently*. To remind, I have to continue to be "it" myself—devoted to being *all in*. To remind, I have to also show up in the coaching hub, reminding you and myself that it is a choice—sometimes daily—to denounce the victim, to defy the fear, to leave behind the old limits of how much goodness you can accept coming to, and flowing through, you.

How about you? How much can you hold? What is yours to create? Who are you to be? What is your destiny?

It might come as a surprise to you that what you are meant to do, is what you love doing. It's that thing that doesn't feel like work, that you would do anyway. How simple a concept: that you would love what it is that you are here for.

STEP 2: So, what is that for you? Write with a pen longhand. Start with: *What I love doing or being is...*

_____

_____

_____

Continue contemplating, and start your next sentence with: *What I would do even if I wasn't getting paid for it...*

_____

_____

_____

Contemplate also how what you love doing and being is serving others. Start the sentence with: *How what I love doing is serving others is...*

_____

_____

_____

Can you give yourself over to a higher version of yourself—if you weren't coming from competition but from creativity? Start your sentence with: *If I wasn't coming from a competitive mind, but from a creative mind, I would love to...*

_____

_____

_____

Lastly, contemplate what it would feel like to touch and inspire others with all that you have learned on your journey—with all that you are. Ask the question: *If I didn't believe it was impossible how would I love to touch others with what I have learned? What is my story of becoming, my story of awakening?* Then put pen to paper and let the words flow.

_____

_____

_____

_____

_____

_____

BIBLIOGRAPHY

Allen, James. *As a Man Thinketh*. Withington: Savoy, 1902.

Andreas, Connirae, and Steve Andreas. *Heart of the Mind*. Boulder: Real People, 1989.

Bandler, Richard, and John Grinder. *Frogs Into Princes*. Boulder: Real People, 1979.

Bays, Brandon. *The Journey*. London: Harper Collins, 1999.

Behrend, Genevieve. *Your Invisible Power*. Holyoke: Elizabeth Towne, 1921.

Cameron, Julia. *The Artist's Way*. Los Angeles: TarcherPerigee, 1992.

Campbell, Joseph. *A Hero with a Thousand Faces*. New York: Pantheon, 1949.

Chopra, Deepak. *Quantum Healing*. New York: Bantam, 1989.

Colgrove, Melba, Harold H. Bloomfield, and Peter McWilliams. *How to Survive the Loss of a Love*. New York: Bantam, 1977.

Emoto, Masaru. *The Miracle of Water*. New York: Atria, 2007.

Engelhart, Matthew, and Terces Engelhart. *Sacred Commerce*. Berkley: North Atlantic, 2008.

A Course in Miracles. Mill Valley: Foundation for Inner Peace, 1975.

Gibran, Kahlil, *The Prophet*. Orig. Publ. 1923. New York: Borzoi, 1973.

Hasselmann, Varda, and Frank Schmolke. *Die Seelenfamilie*. Munich: Goldman, 2013.

Hawkins, David R. *Power Vs. Force*. Sedona: Veritas, 1995.

James, Tad, and Wyatt Woodsmall. *Time Line Therapy*. Capitola: Meta, 1988.

Kotsos, Tania. *The Adventure of I*. London: Amarantho, 2013.

Lipton, Bruce. *Biology of Belief*. Carlsbad: Hay House, 2005.

Michel, Francisca B. *Breaking Out Gently*. Bloomington: Balboa Press/Hay House, 2019.

Pert, Candace B. *Molecules of Emotion*. New York: Scribner, 1997.

Riso, Don Richard, and Ross Hudson. *Personality Types: Using the Enneagram for Self-Discovery*. New York: Mariner, 1996.

Rudd, Richard. *Gene Keys*. London: Watkins, 2009.

Spiller, Jan. *Astrology for the Soul*. New York: Bantam, 1997.

Trine, Ralph Waldo. *In Tune with the Infinite*. London: George Bell & Sons, 1903.

Wattles, Wallace. *The Science of Getting Rich.* Holyoke: Elizabeth Towne, 1910.

Wilder, Barbara. *Money is Love.* Boulder: Wild Ox, 1998

Wing, R. L. *Das Arbeitsbuch zum I Ging.* Munich: Wilhelm Heyne, 1980.

Yogananda, Paramahansa. *Man's Eternal Quest.* Los Angeles: Self-Realization Fellowship, 1982.

Other Books by Francisca B. Michel
Breaking Out Gently

For the Bliss Keys coaching hub, and products
from Francisca B. Michel or to contact her, go to:

Bliss Keys—Unlock Your Purpose
www.BlissKeys.com

Printed in the United States
By Bookmasters